HOME WINE MAKING
BREWING & OTHER DRINKS

HOME WINE MAKING
BREWING & OTHER DRINKS

Charles Foster

A GARDEN WAY BOOK

CONTENTS

Acknowledgement
The author and publishers would like to thank Trevor Haywood of Real Pictures for providing the colour photographs in this book.

Note to American Edition
This is an English book, and, in offering it to our American readers, we at Garden Way are trying to preserve its British flavour.

Thus flavor is spelled flavour, you will be advised to purchase some supplies at chemists, rather than drug stores, recipes call for caster sugar rather than confectioners' sugar, and for sultanas rather than pale yellow, seedless raisins.

Other English expressions are crown caps, instead of bottle caps, to place on bottles. Maize syrup is corn syrup, but golden syrup can be bought in this country. Yeast is "pitched," rather than added, in several recipes.

We have made one major change. A British gallon is larger than an American one – 277.42 cubic inches to 231 cubic inches. And fluid ounces change in size between continents. We have translated all of these into American. To do less would be to discourage the most dedicated before a single grape were crushed.

We have left intact the metric measurements. The reader should follow either the metric or the U.S. measurement throughout a recipe. Do not use a combination of measurements. Although they are usually equal, there are instances where another size, because it is more readily available, is given. For example, 25/litre/5 gallon fermentation jars are recommended even though a 25 litre jar will hold 6½ gallons.

INTRODUCTION

It is reliably estimated that more than three million people now make their own wine or brew their own beer. They have found it not only easy to do but also rewarding in the results obtained. Modern equipment, methods and ingredients have so simplified the processes that everyone can now participate–even the most impractical. The wines being made at home are often as good as, and sometimes even better than, the everyday wines bought in jumbo bottles. The beers, too, are mostly of fine quality and frequently more satisfying than many commercial beers.

There is also a massive saving in cost, since comparable commercial wines and beers can be up to ten times more expensive than those made at home. Much of this cost is in Excise Duty and VAT. Happily, wines and beers may be made freely at home in Britain without registration, licence or tax, provided they are for your own consumption or that of your family or friends. Only if you want to sell your beverages do you need a licence to do so. The definition of selling in this context, however, extends to raffles, tombolas and the like, for which money is paid. It is, therefore, illegal to donate bottles of home-made wine, beer, cider, mead or liqueurs to such fund-raising activities.

Federal regulations in the United States allow an adult to produce not more than 100 gallons per year; a household of two or more adults, 200 gallons yearly for family consumption is the limit. There is no payment of tax required but you must obtain Form 1541 from the U.S. Treasury Department, Internal Revenue Service which is to be filled out and sent to your Assistant Regional Commissoner. To produce more than 200 gallons or to sell your product, you must obtain a permit from the Assistant Regional Commissoner (Alcohol and Tobacco Tax).

Apart from the great saving in cost in making wines and beers etc at home, there is the tremendous satisfaction in making a really enjoyable drink. The wine, beer and cider kits so widely available, produce most acceptable beverages with the minimum of trouble and in the shortest possible time. They make an ideal starting point for everyone new to the hobby. More interesting wines can be made even more cheaply, however, by gathering your own ingredients of fruits, flowers and vegetables from the garden and hedgerow; these cost nothing. They can be used to make either traditional country wines or more complex ones mixed with other ingredients, and similar in style to commercial wines.

In most towns and villages in Britain there are associations of wine and beer makers where you can talk with people who have similar interests to yours. They usually meet once a month and listen to lectures and discussions on different aspects of the hobby, followed by an exchange of tastings of their wines and beers. Many of these clubs are affiliated to a regional federation and to the National Association of Wine and Beer Makers. Competitions are held and trophies and certificates awarded for the best wines and beers of their class or style. There is great fellowship to be found in the clubs and the hobby opens up the way to new friends and holidays. The winemaker never forgets that the grape is the traditional source of wine, and trips are organized to the vineyards and wine cellars of Europe and the USA.

Perhaps the most unexpected benefit of home winemaking is that, drunk in moderation every day, wine is actually good for you. Research has shown that a regular consumption of a moderate amount is medically beneficial. It relaxes the nervous system, reduces tension, dilates blood vessels, minimizes cholesterol, stimulates the appetite, enhances digestion, provides those essential trace elements, minerals and vitamins and gives great pleasure at the same time!

MAKING WINE AT HOME

The Importance of Hygiene

Hygiene is of the utmost importance in winemaking. Dirt, grime and stains on utensils need to be removed before they can be safely used, and all equipment and ingredients need to be sterilized to eliminate wild yeasts, fungi, moulds, and bacteria, thereby producing both clean tasting and good wines. Traditionally, this was carried out by boiling or baking; today it can be done more effectively with a readily available substance called sulphite. When dissolved in a liquid, sulphite releases a gas called sulphur dioxide which is a powerful bactericide.

Sulphite is available in two forms – a white crystalline powder known as sodium metabisulphite and a small aspirin-sized tablet known as a Campden tablet. Those new to the hobby are recommended to use the tablets because they release a known quantity of gas. If stored in a cool, dark place, a sulphite solution keeps for several weeks in a sealed bottle. The cost is so minimal however, that it is best to make up a fresh solution for each winemaking session.

Equipment

A very powerful sterilizing agent can be made by crushing four tablets and dissolving them in 600 ml/1¼ pints of cold water. A 2.5 ml/½ teaspoon of citric acid acts as a reinforcing agent and should also be added. This solution may be used to sterilize the inside of every piece of equipment with which the wine may come into contact. For example, it can be poured into a bottle, shaken and then poured into another bottle. The first bottle is thus sterilized and ready for use. The solution should also be poured through your siphon and funnel, swirled round the inside of bins, used for soaking and softening corks, and for soaking the straining bag for a minute before squeezing it. It is sufficient to shake off the surplus moisture and to use the equipment while still wet. It should not be dried or rinsed before use.

Ingredients

It is advisable to wash both fresh and dried fruits in a diluted sulphite solution before use, to kill off the organisms that have settled on them. For this purpose, one tablet dissolved in 5 litres/1 gallon of cold water is normally sufficient; use two tablets if the fruit is over-ripe.

When fruits have to be crushed or cut up, it is best to drop them at once into cold water containing one crushed Campden tablet. Sulphite also prevents the oxidation of the cut surface of the fruit and stops an unpleasant taste from developing in the wine.

When any must has to be left while pectic enzyme is working, it should be protected by one crushed Campden tablet for every 5 litres/1 gallon of must. When fermentation has finished and the wine is removed from its sediment, it should again be protected by one Campden tablet per 5 litres/1 gallon. This prevents both oxidation of the wine and infection from invisible spoilage organisms. This is especially important in wines that have a low acid and/or alcohol content.

Any fruit juice or wine that has been spilt should be wiped up with a cloth dipped in a sulphite solution.

Keeping Records

Although it is not essential to do so, it makes good sense to keep a detailed record of each wine made, ie a note of the ingredients and quantities used, the method followed, the date the wine was started, dates of racking and bottling and a comment on the finished wine. The record can be kept in a book with each wine numbered or on a purpose-produced card punched for keeping in a small loose-leaf file. Alternatively, a large tie-on luggage label can be attached to the bin, then transferred to the fermentation jar, then to the storage jar. At the bottling stage you can use attractive wine labels available in a wide choice of styles or just a tiny price tag with the bare name or number of the wine relating to the same name or number in your record book.

It is most important to keep each wine properly labelled with its name and year. It is otherwise easy to get the wines mixed up so that you select a sweet wine when you want a dry one or a dessert wine when you want an apéritif. The detailed record can also help you to repeat successes or explain the reason for a fault if and when one should appear.

Stages in Winemaking

There are three distinct and separate stages in making wine that can be described in the three words – Preparation, Fermentation and Maturation.

Preparation of fruit includes the selection and gathering of the fruits, the removal of any stalks and stones, and washing, crushing and steeping the fruit for 24 hours in a sulphite solution containing pectic enzyme. For vegetables, it includes the scrubbing of the roots, dicing and boiling them until tender, then cooling them and straining off the liquor.

For flowers, preparation includes removing the petals after picking them, then steeping them for a few days to extract their fragrance.

Preparation is the stage up to the addition of the yeast. Take care to use good quality ingredients and prepare them carefully for best results.

Fermentation is the process in which the sugar is converted to alcohol by the enzymes secreted by the yeast cells. It can be conducted 'on the pulp', ie in the presence of solids in a bin, or in a fermentation jar sealed with an airlock. The period of fermentation begins as soon as the yeast starts working and continues until it stops. This can be because it has converted all the sugar to alcohol and carbon dioxide or until it has produced so much alcohol that it can tolerate no more.

Maturation is the third stage and begins as soon as fermentation is finished and the new wine is racked off its sediment into sterilized jars or bottles. Maturation continues until the wine is drunk and includes any fining, filtering or blending. Some wines mature more quickly than others and are ready within a few months. Others take much longer and may require several years in cool storage to reach their best.

Wine Styles

All the commercial wine styles can be made at home; apéritifs including vermouths, red, white and rosé table wines, sweet table wines for drinking with the sweet course of a meal and dessert wines for drinking after a meal. Sparkling wines are not difficult to make and sherry styles are also popular.

Apéritifs can be low or high in alcohol, ie a light white wine of around 11% or a long fermented sherry type wine around 16%. Dessert wines should also be as strong as the yeast can ferment them and then sweetened to taste. Table wines to drink with a meal should be around 11% for a white or rosé and 12% for a red; any stronger and you soon become inebriated. Sparkling wines should contain no more than 11% alcohol before refermentation, otherwise it might be difficult to get them to sparkle.

Fresh fruit can be made into dry table wines or richer, sweeter and stronger dessert wines. White wines from fruits seem best as dry or sweet table wines or good dessert wines. Dried fruits such as prunes and raisins are good for sherry apéritifs or dessert wines. In general, vegetables such as beetroot, carrots and parsnips make better dessert wines than other styles. Flowers make light and fragrant wines that are often best enjoyed when served medium sweet on their own and without food.

Equipment

Purpose-made equipment is widely available from home-brew centres, chemists, some department stores and large supermarkets. It is light, easy to clean and long lasting. Once you have decided to make wine regularly it is worth buying a wide range of equipment.

You will need:

Polythene bins with lids, also known as fermentation bins. Available in different sizes from 10 litres/2 gallons to 25 litres/5 gallons.

Fermentation jars. The standard size is a nominal 5 litres/ 1 gallon.

Specific gravity hydrometer and a **trial jar.** These are very useful for checking the sugar content in the must prior to fermentation and for determining precisely how much additional sugar is needed to make a wine of a required alcohol content.

Siphon. This is essential for removing the wine from its sediment. It consists of a plastic tube, on one end of which is fitted a J tube or which is blocked and has small holes in the side of the tube just above the block. A small tap can be attached to the other end so that the flow can be turned on or off as required. Some siphons have a small pump fitted to them to save sucking the wine through the tube.

Storage jars. These may be the same as fermentation jars or may be made from glazed earthenware, which is heavier and opaque and, therefore, insulates the wine from rapid changes in temperature. Small wooden casks have too large a ratio of surface to volume and cause the wine to oxidize too rapidly. The minimum size which is safe to use is 30 litres/5 gallons.

Airlocks, also called fermentation traps. These are made in different shapes from either plastic or glass. They must be fitted into a bored cork or rubber bung that can be inserted into the neck of the fermentation vessel. A little water has to be put into the gadget to form the actual lock. Gas coming from the fermentation is able to push its way through the water, but air from the atmosphere is pre-vented from getting into the jar.

Nylon straining bag. This is required for straining out and pressing the solids dry. A small press is useful if large quantities of fruit are to be pressed.

Other equipment. A potato masher can be used to crush soft fruits. A liquidizer is an alternative. For hard fruits such as apples, a stainless steel blade on a shaft which fits into the chuck of an electric drill is helpful for cutting up large quantities. Alternatively, they can be placed, a few at a time, in a polythene bag and hit with a mallet or rolling-pin.

A large wooden or plastic stirring spoon, kitchen scales and polythene funnels of assorted sizes for bottles and jars, a bottle brush to scrub the inside of bottles and jars, a large stew pan, fish kettle or preserving pan for boiling vegetables will also be needed. These may indeed already be available.

Bottles. A good stock of proper wine bottles should be assembled, soaked until the labels slide off, washed clean and sterilized with sulphite. Suitable cylindrical corks will be needed together with a simple corking tool to drive them into the necks of the bottles. There are several types available.

Champagne bottles are essential for sparkling wines, together with hollow-domed stoppers and wire cages to fasten them on. Plastic or foil capsules are available for covering the top of the cork and neck of the bottle, together with decorative labels and shoulder bands to provide a professional finish.

Ingredients

There are a number of essential ingredients in the making of wine: water, sugar, yeast, acid, nutrient and flavouring for example. It is important to include them all to obtain a good balance in the finished wine although the precise quantity of each is not critical. The figures given in the recipes on pages 29–51 are more of a guide than a meticulous instruction. It is, however, important not to make a substantial addition to the sugar quantities since the amount of alcohol formed must be relevant to the style of wine. This is particularly important when making sparkling wines for which the sugar quantity must be accurate.

Water is by far the largest component, comprising some 85–90% of the total volume. Some of it may come in the form of fruit juice but much of it comes from the tap. In the United Kingdom this is pure and may safely be used without first boiling it unless the water is heavily chlorinated or fluorided. Where necessary, the water should be boiled to drive off the chlorine and fluoride which would otherwise inhibit the fermentation. The softness or hardness of the water seems not to have any noticeable effect on the quality of the finished wine. Spring water is good and well water may also be used, provided it is safe for drinking. Rain water must be boiled and filtered before use.

Sugar, whether naturally present in the fruit or added as granulated white sugar, is the source of the alcohol that gives wine its special satisfaction. Brown sugars may be used when trying to create a Madeira type wine with a caramelized taste, but the flavour of brown sugar is distinctive and can spoil other wine styles. Glucose and/or fructose may be used as an alternative to white sugar, as can golden syrup or honey. The latter two, which contain only 75% sugar, impart their own special flavour, however, which may not always be wanted. Caster sugar is generally used for priming sparkling wine as it dissolves more rapidly, but granulated sugar is also suitable. Approximately two-thirds of the weight of sultanas and raisins, and about half the weight of jam or jelly, consist of fermentable sugars.

Yeast is the invisible botanical cell that secretes a number of enzymes which cause the conversion of sugar to alcohol and carbon dioxide. There are a thousand different varieties, only a few of which are beneficial in the making of alcoholic drinks.

Only pure wine yeasts should be used for making wine; baker's and brewer's yeasts are not suitable as they impart an off flavour and do not settle cleanly after fermentation. Wine yeasts are available in many sub varieties suitable for making different styles of wine, eg champagne, sherry, port etc. They are mostly available in a dormant condition in the form of dried granules or tablets in a sealed sachet to keep them in a good condition. A drumful of loose granules may be bought but these tend to deteriorate if kept for more than six months. Yeasts can sometimes be bought in a tiny phial of distilled water or on a slant of agar in a sealed test tube. One German manufacturer markets a wide range of dried yeasts on slivers of dried rose-hip shells.

Acid and nutrient are also needed. The acid is required not only for the yeast, but also to enhance the bouquet and flavour of the wine. Yeast can only function efficiently in a mildly acid solution. The three acids most commonly used are citric, malic and tartaric. Citric acid is cheapest and stimulates a good fermentation. Malic acid imparts a fresh fruity taste, but is easily converted by bacteria into the less sharp tasting lactic acid. Tartaric acid is found only in grapes and is sometimes precipitated as cream of tartar crystals, especially if the storage vessel is left in too cold a position. Most fruits contain some acid although dates have almost none, while lemons and blackcurrants have plenty. Vegetables, flowers and honey contain no acid, and between 15 ml/1 tablespoon and 30 ml/2 tablespoons per 5 litres/1 gallon may have to be added depending on the style of wine being made. Dry light wines need less acid than sweet strong wines.

Nutrient in the context of winemaking is just another name for nitrogen. The yeast cannot ferment and thrive without the aid of some nitrogen. Usually, it obtains this from the fruit or vegetable, but flowers and honey contain no nitrogenous material, and it is, therefore, necessary to add some. Even when fruit is fermented on the pulp, it is wise to include a small quantity of nutrient, say 2.5 ml/ ½ teaspoon per 5 litres/1 gallon. This is especially so if a dry wine is required and even more so, if a really strong wine is wanted. If the yeast has to work particularly hard it needs all the support it can get.

Nutrient is usually in the form of a white crystalline powder called diammonium phosphate; sometimes a nutrient mixture also contains some ammonium sulphate and thiamine or vitamin B.

Flavouring is provided from the different fruits, flowers and vegetables used. The better the quality of the ingredient, the better the wine. The flavour is best extracted by crushing the fruit and soaking it for 24 hours in the presence of some pectic enzyme. By fermenting the fruit on the pulp even more flavour, colour and constituents are released.

Some fruits such as elderberries, blackberries, damsons, plums and sloes benefit by having hot water poured over them. This helps to extract the colour. Some hard fruits too difficult to crush, may be softened with hot water, then crushed when cool. Fruits should never be boiled since this often causes a haze in the wine. Dried fruits such as prunes, apricots and figs need to be washed, broken and then steeped in hot water overnight. Stones should be removed from all fruits since these impart an unpleasant flavour to the wine.

Generally speaking, the fruit needs to be just ripe; neither under-ripe since it is then too acid, nor so over-ripe that portions are beginning to deteriorate or become mouldy. The one exception to this is the banana. This is best for winemaking when the skins are well spotted or even thin and dark brown. These are discarded and the soft, even brownish fruit can be easily sliced or mashed and added to the must.

Citrus fruits must be very thinly pared, removing and retaining only the coloured rind containing the zest. The white pith is very pectinous and imparts an extremely bitter taste to the wine. The expressed and strained juice is also

A selection of bottles suitable for winemaking.

used. Pineapples must be topped, tailed and washed free from dust etc, but need not be peeled before crushing or chopping up.

The quantity of fruit to use varies with the intensity of flavour of the fruit and the style of wine being made. For example, from 4 kg/8 lb to 5 kg/10 lb apples are needed to flavour and give body to 5 litres/1 gallon of table wine in contrast to only 1 kg/2 lb elderberries. Dessert wines need both more flavour and body and this can often best be obtained by using a mixture of different fruits. Bananas and dried fruit are good for adding body and enhancing flavour.

Fruit that has been frozen and stored in a home freezer is ideal for making wine. During the freezing process the crystals of ice formed in the juice burst the walls of the cell structure, making the fruit easier to crush and thereby ensuring better juice extraction. Before putting the fruit in the freezer, it should be washed, stalked and stoned, then steeped for one minute in a sulphite solution. After draining away the solution the fruit should be packed into vapourproof polythene containers or thick polythene bags and securely tied at the neck to exclude air. This basic preparation eliminates the likelihood of oxidation when the fruit is thawing. It can then be used in exactly the same way as fresh fruit.

Canned fruits in syrup make good light wines, as does unsweetened fruit juice.

Vegetables are at their best when used fairly early in the season from maincrop varieties. If they can be freshly dug, so much the better. They should be topped and tailed, scrubbed thoroughly clean, then sliced or diced and boiled in a closed pan until soft but not mushy. After leaving them to cool, the liquor should be strained out and used to make the wine; the vegetables can be eaten or discarded. Vegetable wines often take two years or more to mature and develop an attractive flavour; they are particularly good when made sweet and strong.

Flowers should be picked on a dry sunny day when they are fully open. When gathered from the hedgerow, they should be taken home in paper rather than in plastic bags, since the latter causes them to sweat and makes the removal of the petals very difficult. All trace of green stem, leaf and calyx should be removed since this causes a

Equipment for making wine is easily available from home-brew centres,
chemists, department stores and large supermarkets.

bitterness in the wine. The petals should be steeped in hot water and rubbed against the side of the container with the back of a wooden spoon to extract their fragrance. They should then be left to steep under a cover, protected by one crushed Campden tablet per 5 litres/1 gallon must for two or three days, rubbing the petals twice each day. As with vegetables, the infusion should be strained out and used, and the petals discarded.

Vine and bramble shoots from summer pruning must be washed, chopped small and steeped in hot water as for fruit wines.

Herbs are not much used in making wines nowadays since our wines are made for social rather than medicinal purposes. Packets of herb flavourings to make vermouth type wines can be bought in some shops and instructions for their use are given on the packet. Tea leaves and coffee beans have been used by some winemakers but the results are generally not very satisfactory. Ginger is occasionally used for flavouring marrow and other bland wines but is not as good as the many fruit-based wines that can so easily be made.

Experience has shown that the addition of some grape in one form or another to all wines greatly improves the vinosity and body of the wine. When making 5 litres/1 gallon of a table wine it is wise to include 1 kg/2 lb fresh grapes, picked from their stalks, washed and crushed, or 250 g/8 oz concentrated grape juice or 250 g/8 oz washed and chopped sultanas or raisins or 600 ml/20 oz of bottled grape juice. As much again can be included in dessert wines since these need more than table wines.

Pectolytic enzyme (pectic enzyme) is recommended when making wine from fruit to dissolve the natural pectin content. It also helps to extract all the juice and flavour in addition to preventing a pectin haze in the finished wine. The enzyme is available both as a brown liquid and as a white powder. One 5 ml spoon/1 teaspoon of either form is usually adequate when making 5 litres/1 gallon of fruit wine, whether fresh, frozen, canned or dried. Pectic enzyme is not required when making wine from concentrates, flowers, grains, herbs, honey or vegetables.

Tannin is frequently added to certain wines to give them character and a hint of bitterness. Grape tannin in powder or liquid form made from the skins, pips and stalks of grapes should be used. Black grapes, elderberries and pears have sufficient tannin in their skins and rarely need any addition. Some other black fruits, eg blackberries and damsons, contain a modest quantity. White wines need less tannin than red. The recommended addition for 5 litres/1 gallon of must is 2.5–5 ml/½–1 teaspoon tannin.

Campden tablets are not an ingredient but a bactericide. Their mention in the recipes is a reminder to use them to protect the must during any steeping periods and again upon the first racking.

Potassium sorbate is sometimes used to terminate fermentation so as to produce a sweet wine with a moderate rather than a high alcohol content. It must be used in conjunction with Campden tablets, the dose being 1.25 ml/¼ teaspoon potassium sorbate and 1 Campden tablet per 5 litres/1 gallon must.

Finings Few wines need finings since most of them clear naturally. If a faint haze does remain however, finings may be added about one month after the first racking. There are several proprietary brands available. Most are based on dissolved isinglass although bentonite gel is also effective. Instructions for their use are provided with the fining agent.

Temperature

This is a particularly important factor in winemaking, especially at the fermentation stage. Yeast is fairly tolerant of heat and will ferment in the range 10°–30°C/50°–86°F. At temperatures lower than 10°C/50°F, activity is sluggish and eventually stops, although the yeast is not killed. At temperatures higher than 30°C/86°F, fermentation also becomes sluggish and eventually stops. Some yeasts are killed at 40°C/104°F and they all die at 50°C/122°F. Around 21°C/70°F seems the optimum temperature for the best results, especially for red wines. White wines, however, seem to retain greater flavour if fermented at around 15°C/59°F. In cold weather, thermal belts, pads and boxes may be used to maintain a steady temperature. An immersion heater coupled to a thermostat may also be used, but many of these are regulated at 24°C/75°F which is rather on the high side for quality wines. In hot weather, it may be necessary to stand a jar of fermenting must in a large bowl of cold water, and to cover it with a wet linen cloth with the ends dangling in the water.

GUIDE TO WINEMAKING

Wines from Kits

Probably more wine is made from kits than from anything else. Each kit comes with step-by-step instructions, and all the winemaker has to provide is some sugar, the water and, generally, the Campden tablets. Some kits even come complete with equipment. The wines mature quickly – some in as little as a few weeks, others in a few months. This is an ideal way for someone new to the hobby to begin since it is an easy way to familiarize oneself with hygiene, fermentation, racking and bottling. It is also a very convenient way for those with limited storage facilities.

The essential equipment is a 5 litre/1 gallon fermentation jar and another one for storage, an airlock and bored bung, an unbored bung, a siphon and a plastic funnel plus wine bottles and corks.

Different wine styles need slightly different treatment. There is a wide choice available of white table wines – Bordeaux, Hock, Sauternes and Moselle styles, and dry red table wines – Claret, Burgundy and Beaujolais styles. A slightly sweet rosé, a range of vermouth sherry, port and Madeira styles, as well as some fruit wines including apricot, blackcurrant and cherry are also obtainable.

The basic principle of hygiene remains the same for kits as it does for all winemaking. The main difference, however, is the overall timing which is considerably shorter. There is no initial fermenting on the pulp in a polythene bin; instead, the must which is made of concentrated grape juice compound is poured straight into the fermentation jar, together with water and the yeast granules provided. This fermenting must is left in a warm place for between seven and ten days. A cooled sugar syrup is then added to the jar and the must left until fermentation is complete -- another three to four weeks.

The wine is then siphoned off its deposit of sediment into a sterilized storage jar, topped up with cold boiled water, sterilized with a Campden tablet, bunged tight and left for another six to eight weeks until mature. It is then siphoned into bottles, corked and labelled. The first bottle will be ready to drink after a further two weeks.

Do not wait until the first wine is mature before starting on another. If you aim to drink only one bottle a week, you need to start on a new kit at least every six weeks. Better still, widen your range of styles so that you have a choice of wines. Have some sherry/vermouth that you keep for apéritifs, dry red and white table wines to accompany different foods, rosé for picnics, parties or snacks, dessert wines to follow the meal and, finally, something slightly different with perhaps a distinctive fruit base, to use as a talking point or for a welcome to a visiting friend. Think about your needs and make your wines accordingly.

Fruit, vegetables and other wine flavourings should be of top quality. This will ensure very superior wines. Other winemaking ingredients such as Campden tablets, wine yeasts and citric acid are obtainable from home-brew centres and large stores.

Making Fresh and Dried Fruit Table Wines

As stated earlier, choose unblemished fruits whenever possible that are just ripe and in perfect condition. If it is necessary to use damaged fruit – windfall apples for example – cut away and discard the bruised and blemished parts. The fruit actually used must be in good condition if you want to make good wine. If possible, use a mixture of different varieties of the same fruit. Balance the acidity and flavour of the fruit with other ingredients. For example, when using elderberries which lack acid but which have a very strong flavour, include some apples, blackberries, blackcurrants, cherries or damsons. Dried figs and apricots have a very strong flavour and 275–375 g/10–13 oz per 5 litres/1 gallon is plenty. Make up the body with bananas, rose-hips or sultanas.

GENERAL GUIDE TO PULP FERMENTATION

1) Select and prepare the fruit.
2) Add one crushed Campden tablet, the acid and pectic enzyme to cold water in a sterilized polythene bin.
3) Add the prepared fruit.
4) Cover and leave for 24 hours in a warm place.
   Alternatively
   Pour hot water over the prepared fruit from which the colour has to be extracted, cover and leave to cool. Then add pectic enzyme, any acid needed and one crushed Campden tablet per 5 litres/1 gallon of wine. Replace the cover and leave the must for 24 hours.
5) Stir the must well, strain out a sample through a fine sieve or piece of nylon and pour it into a trial jar in which the hydrometer has already been placed. As soon as the hydrometer is floating freely, record the specific gravity reading on it. This indicates the natural sugar content of the must. Due to a condition known as surface tension, the must will reach a little way up the side of the hydrometer and trial jar, in a saucer shape. The figure to record is at the bottom of the saucer. The temperature of the must should be 15°C/59°F; if it is higher, additions should be made to the figure recorded (see the chart on p19). Return the sample to the bin after recording the reading.

Above *Checking the specific gravity of a must. A reading of 1.080 is suitable for most table wines.*

Below *Yeast should be activated in a sterilized bottle and plugged with cotton wool (see page 18).*

6) Add tannin where required, an activated yeast and nutrient.
Note To activate the yeast, pour the contents of a sachet of yeast into a sterilized standard size wine or similar bottle containing 150–300 ml/5–10 oz of cold boiled water, and swirl the yeast round until dissolved. Loosely plug the neck of the bottle with cotton wool and leave it in a temperature of 40°C/104°F for a few hours. Agitate the contents of the bottle from time to time by shaking gently. Within 4–24 hours the water will turn milky and bubbles will be seen rising to the surface. This is proof that the yeast is rehydrated and viable. It is at this point that the contents are added to the must to start the main fermentation.

If the sachet of yeast does not contain citric acid, ammonium sulphate and sugar, or if a yeast tablet or a liquid yeast is used, add it to 300 ml/10 oz of cold boiled water together with the juice of half an orange and 5 ml/1 teaspoon of caster sugar. Pour this into the sterilized starter bottle and continue as described above.

7) Cover the bin and leave it in a temperature of about 21°C/70°F for 24 hours.

8) Next day, check that fermentation has started and stir well. If the fruit is not floating on top of the water, then fermentation has not started and you must wait another day. Once it has started, keep the pulp submerged or press it down once or twice a day; a china plate is very useful for this purpose. The container should be kept well covered throughout, although the fermentation gas must be allowed to escape.

9) Between three and seven days after fermentation has started, strain out, press dry and discard the fruit. When pressing, use a steady pressure with intermediate pauses rather than continuous pressure. After a while, stir up the fruit pulp, then resume pressing. In this way, up to 80% of the weight of the fruit can be extracted. With apples, for example, it is quite possible to start with 50 kg/100 lb of crushed apples and to finish with a pressed apple cake weighing no more than 10 kg/20 lb. Soft fruits such as grapes, blackcurrants, ripe peaches, plums etc may do even better!

Immediately after use, sterilize and wash out the pressing cloths and press before putting them away.
Note You need not always discard the pressed fruit cake, but can sometimes use it to make a second-run wine. For example, apple wine and elderberry wine are often made at about the same time. After taking your first pressing from each, put the two pressed cakes, well broken up, into a bin and add tepid water (about 21°C/70°F). Stir thoroughly, add some acid, sugar and concentrated rosé grape juice, cover and leave in a warm place for one week, keeping the pulp submerged. You will produce quite a useful rosé wine for everyday drinking as well as the separate apple and elderberry wines.

GENERAL GUIDE TO SECONDARY FERMENTATION

When all the solids have been removed from the must, extra sugar usually has to be added to ensure that the finished wine will have the required alcoholic strength. For instance, if a dry table wine containing 12% alcohol is required, a must containing 1.4 kg/2 lb 6 oz sugar in 5 litres/1 gallon is needed. A hydrometer expresses this as a specific gravity (SG) of 1.090. It is true to say that the more sugar that is added, the more alcohol will normally be formed, up to the alcoholic tolerance of the yeast. But alcohol alone does not make good wine, and too much spoils it.
Note Within the recipes which follow on pages 29–51, the correct quantity of sugar has, in most cases, been calculated, thereby making the use of a hydrometer unnecessary.

Experience shows that a must will ferment best if the initial specific gravity is no higher than 1.090. If a stronger wine is required, as in sherry or port types, then enough extra sugar needs to be added when the specific gravity falls to just below 1.010 to increase the reading to 1.020 (see pages 23 and 24).

The following tables show the approximate quantity of alcohol by volume that can be produced from a given quantity of sugar.

Specific gravity	potential % alcohol	Weight of sugar per 5 litres	1 gallon	
		grams	lb	oz
1.010	0.9	60		2
1.015	1.6	120		4
1.020	2.3	180		6
1.025	3.0	245		8
1.030	3.7	305		11
1.035	4.4	365		13
1.040	5.1	430		15
1.045	5.8	490	1	2
1.050	6.5	550	1	3
1.055	7.2	610	1	5
1.060	7.8	670	1	7
1.065	8.6	730	1	10
1.070	9.2	795	1	12
1.075	9.9	855	1	14
1.080	10.6	920	2	
1.085	11.3	980	2	2
1.090	12.0	1040	2	5
1.095	12.7	1100	2	7
1.100	13.4	1160	2	9
1.105	14.1	1220	2	11
1.110	14.9	1285	2	13
1.115	15.6	1345	2	15
1.120	16.3	1410	3	2
1.125	17.0	1470	3	4
1.130	17.7	1530	3	6
1.135	18.4	1590	3	8

If the temperature of the must varies from 15°C/59°F, then adjustment has to be made to the figures as follows:

Temperature °C	°F	Correction to the last figure of the specific gravity reading
10	50	Subtract 0.6
15	59	No correction necessary
20	68	Add 0.9
25	77	Add 2.0
30	86	Add 3.4
35	95	Add 5.0
40	104	Add 6.8

Table wines taste best when they contain no more than 12% alcohol by volume, and for this reason the total quantity of sugar needs to be closely controlled and limited. Deduct the original specific gravity of the must from that required to produce the right amount of alcohol and add the sugar represented by the difference. For example, if the initial specific gravity of a must is 1.020 and the gravity required is 1.090, the difference of .070 requires the addition of 795 g/1 lb 12 oz sugar.

When the approximately correct quantity of sugar has been stirred into the strained must, pour it into a sterilized fermentation jar, top up with cold boiled water if necessary, fit an airlock and leave the jar in a warm position. To produce a dry wine with a specific gravity of 0.996, leave until fermentation is complete (this step is known as fermenting out).

For a sweet table wine, terminate the fermentation at a given point, eg SG 1.016, instead of allowing the fermentation to end naturally.

Note The alcohol is formed by the reduction of the sugar molecules. This is caused by the presence of enzymes secreted by the active yeast cells. The sugar molecule is composed of carbon, hydrogen and oxygen and is one of the many carbohydrates which are the enemy of all slimmers. The alcohol molecule is also composed of carbon, hydrogen and oxygen but has fewer carbon and oxygen atoms than the sugar. The latter combine to form carbon dioxide which rises in small bubbles to the surface of the must during fermentation and burst with a soft hissing sound. In fact, the rising bubbles are the visible indication of fermentation, and the hissing is the audible sign.

Stuck ferments

Although it is not common, musts can stop fermenting before all the sugar is converted into alcohol. This is known as a stuck ferment and can be caused by the yeast cells being inhibited by extremes of heat or cold, by the absence of acid or nutrient and by carbon dioxide which cannot escape.

If a fermentation sticks, the must should firstly be aerated thoroughly by giving it a good stir or by pouring it into another container. In this way, carbon dioxide is pushed out and fresh air containing oxygen is absorbed to revive the yeast cells and so start them reproducing themselves again. A change of temperature may also be necessary, from a cooler to a warmer spot or vice versa. Some extra acid and nutrient may also be needed to get fermentation started again, but your records should be checked first. If all else fails, it may be necessary to start off a new yeast and when it is thoroughly active to add the "stuck" must to the active yeast in small quantities. For example, make up half a bottle of yeast starter, then top it up with "stuck" must. When the bottle is fermenting thoroughly, add it to another bottle of "stuck" must. When this quantity is moving, add it to another two bottles and so on until the total quantity is fermenting again.

Airlocks are made in different shapes, all of which are equally suitable for making wine. They may be fitted into either bored or rubber bungs.

GENERAL GUIDE TO MATURATION

When the visible signs of fermentation stop, ie when no more bubbles can be seen rising in the wine or passing through the airlock, the wine begins to mature. During the following months and even years, further chemical changes take place. Acids are converted, aldehydes are formed, tartrates are deposited, the wine clears, and harshness gives place to smoothness. A poor smell and taste gradually improve out of all recognition into an attractive bouquet and a delightful flavour. How long this takes varies with each individual wine, and the manner in which it is treated.

1) **Racking.** As soon as fermentation is finished, remove the wine from the sediment (lees) which becomes clearly visible on the bottom of the jar as the wine begins to clear. The sediment contains fruit pulp, dead and living yeast cells, micro-organisms of various kinds, and a multitude of bits, pieces and even dust! The clearing wine can sometimes just be poured off into a clean vessel, but this is not easy to do without disturbing the sediment. By far the easiest way is to siphon the wine into a sterilized jar, as follows:

   a) Place the wine to be racked on a high stool or table and place the sterilized jar to be filled immediately below it.

   b) Carefully immerse a siphon in the wine without disturbing the sediment.

   c) Place the other end in the mouth and suck until the tube is full of wine.

   d) Grip the tube firmly to prevent the wine escaping and place the end in the storage jar. Pressure on the tube is then released and the wine starts flowing steadily.

   e) As the level of the wine goes down, tilt the top jar slowly and carefully so that the clear wine slides gently over the sediment and is sucked into the siphon.

   f) At the point when the sediment reaches the siphon, return the jar to the upright position and remove the siphon.

   Note Early maturing wines such as those made from canned fruit, are best racked into bottles as soon as they are clear.

2) **Topping up.** As there is always some wastage when racking because the sediments are discarded, the storage jar will not be quite full. It should therefore be topped up, preferably with wine of the same or a similar kind. Any excess quantity of must produced and fermented in a bottle beside the jar is ideal for topping up. If wine is not available, a little cold boiled water should be used. It is very important always to keep jars full, otherwise micro-organisms in the air may settle on the surface of the wine. Some may form a floury looking skin – called flowers of wine. This eventually reduces the alcohol to carbon dioxide and water. Other microbes may convert the alcohol to vinegar.

3) To inhibit further fermentation, add one crushed Campden tablet to each 5 litres/1 gallon of wine. This stabilizes the wine, protects it from infection and oxidation and helps to improve the flavour and clarity. For a sweet table wine, add 1.25 ml/¼ teaspoon potassium sorbate with the Campden tablet. Alternatively, ferment a full bodied wine to dryness and add saccharin or a little sugar syrup just before the wine is to be served.

4) Insert a clean, sterilized and softened cork or bung in the neck of the storage jar and press firmly home.

5) Label the jar with a note of its contents, the date the wine was started and the date it was racked. Unless it is your only wine, you will soon forget which jar contains what and when it was racked.

Right When racking wine, it is important to place the jars on different levels, as shown.

STORAGE

A cool, still and dark store is now required for the next stage. Suitable places to store wine vary from home to home. A spare bedroom, a large cupboard or wardrobe, the space under the stairs, a garage or outhouse, the space under the floorboards, all these are in use by different winemakers. Temperature changes in a loft vary too frequently and too drastically and cannot therefore be recommended. Bottle cartons can be stacked together on their sides for the storage of bottles. Jars are usually stored upright, preferably on shelves adequately wide and suitably spaced for height.

After about 6–8 weeks the wine should be fairly bright, but if it remains hazy, mix in some finings. Re-cork the storage jar and leave it for a week or two in as cold a place as possible before racking the wine again; it should then be brilliantly clear. Continue to store the wine in bulk for another two or three months at least before bottling it. Strong dessert wines need much longer than table wines, preferably a year or, better still, two.

If you wish to store large quantities of wine in a cask, the following preparation must be carried out:

1) Soak the cask in water until all the staves are tight.
2) Fill it with hot water containing a handful of washing soda.
3) Roll the cask about and leave it until the water is cool, then empty it and rinse with clean, cold water.
4) Mix up a solution of eight Campden tablets and 5 ml/ 1 teaspoon of citric acid in 1 litre/2 pints of tepid water. Pour this into the cask, fit the bung and swirl the solution around and around the inside of the cask for several minutes. Ensure that every crack and crevice is well soaked with the solution.
5) Drain the cask dry, then add half a bottle of the wine that is to be stored in the cask. Swirl this also around and around the cask to season the timber.
6) Drain the cask dry, discarding the wine used and set the cask up on a cradle so that the belly staves are not in contact with the floor or shelf.
7) Fill the cask with the new wine, right to the bung hole, bung tight and pin a label on to the cask showing the name and date of the wine.

8) Check the level of the wine every two weeks and, if necessary, top the cask up with wine similar to that already in it. A certain amount of evaporation takes place and in a humid atmosphere alcohol is also lost. Excessive air in the cask will cause the wine to oxidize and impart an unpleasant taste, so it is important always to keep the cask full to the bung. In small casks, six months' maturation is usually long enough before bottling the wine.

Note Do not store wine in a cask with a capacity of less than 25 litres/5 gallons.

BLENDING

The greatest mistake of the majority of winemakers is the belief that all their 'geese are swans'. Far too many are satisfied with wines of indifferent quality that could be vastly improved by blending. They feel that it is an admission of failure to blend their wines! Commercial winemakers and brokers almost always blend wines in the knowledge that each wine has something to give to the other. Indeed, this is the vintner's art. Only superb wines and contaminated wines should not be blended. The latter should be discarded.

When a wine is thought to be ready for bottling, taste it and decide whether to bottle it as it is or to blend it with another. If your standards are high enough and you decide to blend, choose an opposite type of wine to mix it with. For example, if one is too sweet, then choose another that is too dry. If one is too acid, then choose another that tastes medicinal. If one tastes too rough and harsh, then choose another that is too soft and flabby. You need not be afraid to mix red with white, to form a rosé. If you have all the six types mentioned, then blend them all together!

Pour the wines into a large plastic bin or suitable container, stir them up, wash the individual jars, drain them and pour the blended wine back into them. If possible, fit an airlock containing a little sulphite solution in each jar, and leave for a few days; if you have insufficient airlocks, use cotton wool plugs. Quite frequently, a further fermentation takes places as the wine homogenizes. If fermentation does not occur within 48 hours, add one Campden tablet per 5 litres/1 gallon of wine. A deposit is often thrown and racking is then necessary when the wine clears. However, after a few months in a jar, followed by a few more in a bottle, you will be surprised at the improvement that has taken place in the wine.

BOTTLING

When suitably mature, and, if necessary, blended and/or sweetened with saccharin, siphon the wine into proper wine bottles which have been thoroughly washed inside and out as follows:

Remove any old labels, scrub the inside of the bottles with a bottle brush, especially in the punt, rinse and drain, then sterilize with a sulphite solution. Soak new cylindrical corks in the same sterilizing solution for 24 hours, making sure that they are kept well under the surface of the solution. Drain them just before use. Siphon the mature wine into the bottles up to the bottom of the neck, leaving a space of about 2.5 cm/1 inch between the surface of the wine and the bottom of the cork.

With the aid of a simple corking tool, drive a cork into the neck of each bottle, and fit a viscap or foil cover of red, gold or silver over the cork. Label the bottles with the name and date of the wine and store them on their side in a cool place for another few months, depending on their style.

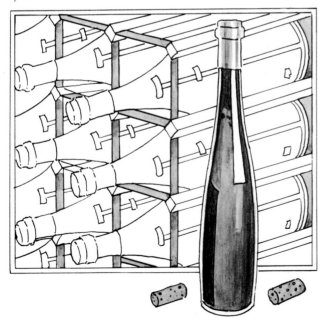

Making Dessert Wines

Most dessert wines are of a port or Madeira type. They are made in the same way as table wines but with additional body, acid and flavour. A high alcohol-tolerant yeast should be used such as a port, Madeira or Tokay, and some additional yeast nutrient should be included in the must, plus one 3 mg tablet of vitamin B_1. Extra sugar is added in small doses during fermentation to increase the alcohol content to the maximum that can be tolerated by the yeast; this should be added as follows:

After recording the initial specific gravity, remove some of the must, dissolve half the extra sugar in it, then return the must to the jar and again check and record the specific gravity. Repeat with half the rest of the sugar a week later and finally with the last batch of sugar a week later still. By adding together the total number of units fermented, the approximate alcohol content can be ascertained from the table on page 19.

After racking, dessert wines can be sweetened with sugar to taste but must be matured for several years. A Campden tablet need not be added since the wine will be protected by its high alcohol content.

Dessert wines may be fortified with vodka of approximately 40% alcohol at the rate of one bottle of spirit to five bottles of wines as soon as the fermentation is finished and the wine is bright. This increases the alcohol of the wine by about 4%. Since a fortified dessert wine needs to be sweet, you can adjust the sugar content to around SG 1.020 or above at the same time as you add the spirit because the alcohol will inhibit further fermentation. Fortified wines need to have at least two or three years' maturation before they are ready to drink. Keep them in bulk for at least two years before bottling and for at least another year afterwards. Even then, they may not be quite ready, depending on the amount of acid, tannin, alcohol and flavour in the wine. All are necessary to balance one another. Such wines usually contain about 20% alcohol by volume.

The neck of a fermentation jar containing a sherry-type wine should be plugged with cotton wool. This ensures that the wine will have a characteristic sherry aroma and flavour.

Making Sherry-type Wines

These wines should have been fermented by a sherry yeast to the maximum alcohol tolerance, ie 16% or 17%. Instead of an airlock, the neck of the fermentation jar should be plugged with cotton wool as should the storage jar. The wine needs to be matured for at least one year in the jar in which there is a clear headspace over the wine so that it can develop its distinctive oxidized aroma and flavour. The cotton wool allows a little air to enter the jar during contraction of the wine during periods of falling temperature, but filters out airborne micro-organisms.

A dry sherry-type wine should have been fermented for as long as possible with additional doses of sugar in the same way as dessert wines so that the maximum alcohol content has been formed and the wine left dry, ie without any taste of sweetness and with a specific gravity of around 0.994. This wine needs no extra sulphiting since this might inhibit the development of a sherry flor; in any case the wine is protected by the extra alcohol. A flor may develop between three and six months after the finish of fermentation, but this is by no means certain and cannot be induced. It looks like a surface of white dots, criss-crossed by lines. The wine must be kept free from vibration in a temperature of 17°C/65°F and stored for a year under the flor which will impart that distinctive sherry taste to the wine.

A sweet sherry-type wine should be much fuller bodied and have a specific gravity of around 1.020. It will not develop a flor and should be a little stronger than a dry sherry to balance the extra sugar. For this reason you may want to fortify the wine. Do this by adding one bottle of sherry brandy, such as Fundador, to five bottles of the wine after the first racking.

Sherry is always blended and it is beneficial to blend together several sherry-type wines after about a year in bulk storage. A bottle of commercial sherry may also be added at the time of blending to enhance the flavour. The proportion of one to five has proved effective.

Making Sparkling Wines

Excellent sparkling wines can be made from apples, gooseberries, rhubarb, white currants and hard pears. An initial specific gravity of 1.082 is quite high enough. At the end of fermentation, add some proprietary wine finings if necessary and rack when the wine is clear. Do not add a Campden tablet since this may inhibit the secondary fermentation.

A wine to be sparkled should be star-bright, bone dry and about six months old. Activate a Champagne yeast and when it is fermenting vigorously, add it to the six months old wine, together with a precise amount of sugar. For 5 litres use 75 g sugar and for 1 gallon use 2 oz; these figures are quite critical for the best results. More sugar than that recommended will make the wine too gassy and difficult to handle. Less sugar will cause the wine to have too little gas and therefore insufficient sparkle to be attractive.

The specific gravity should always be checked before the addition of the priming sugar to ensure that there is no residual sugar in the wine. A reading of 0.994 is safe. It is also important that the wine should not be too strong; about 11% alcohol is enough. If the wine is stronger it may not be possible to start the priming fermentation. Before adding the sugar, withdraw a little of the wine and dissolve the sugar in it. Caster sugar is recommended because it dissolves more quickly than other kinds, but granulated sugar is also suitable. Return the sweetened wine to the bulk, mix in the activated yeast, fit an airlock and leave the wine in a warm place for a few hours. To stimulate the fermentation, a pinch of nutrient may also be added.

As soon as the wine can be seen to be fermenting, siphon it into sterilized champagne bottles. (Beer, cider and mineral water bottles are not strong enough and should not be used. Ordinary wine bottles are totally unsuitable.) Leave a headspace of about 5 cm/2 inches above the wine and fit hollow-domed or blister stoppers. Fasten them on with a wire cage. Lay the bottles on their sides, in a warm place, for seven days while the sugar is fermenting, then move them to a cool store for a minimum of six months. For some reason not yet fully understood, the wine develops better if the bottles are laid on their side during the secondary fermentation period and maturation than if they are stood upright.

Above *Fitting a hollow-domed stopper on to a champagne bottle.*

Below *Inserting the neck and stopper of a champagne bottle in a container of ice to freeze the sediment.*

At the end of this period, place the bottles, stopper first, in a suitable carton and fix this at an angle of 45°. Each day give each bottle a gentle shake and twist until the sediment has moved from the side of the bottle into the stopper or blister. The latter may now be bent over and fastened with the clip provided to prevent the return of the sediment to the wine. If a hollow-domed stopper has been used, the neck and stopper of the bottle should be inserted into a container of crushed ice and cooking salt, and left for eight to ten minutes. (A dozen ice cubes well crushed and mixed with 30 ml/2 tablespoons of cooking salt is adequate.) It helps if the wine has first been chilled in the refrigerator for an hour or so. Keep the bottle upside-down, of course, or the sediment will move out of the stopper. Home freezers should not be used for this purpose since the intense cold could damage the wine, and, if left too long in the freezer might freeze all the wine and break the bottle.

When the wine in the stopper is frozen, carefully remove the bottle from the ice and return it to the upright position. Remove the cage and ease out the stopper containing its frozen wine and the sediment encapsuled within it. Insert a clean stopper already softened in hot water and replace the cage. The sparkling wine is now ready for serving but may be kept until it is required.

To take the extreme edge of dryness off the wine, add one saccharin tablet to the bottle before inserting the second stopper. Add two tablets to produce a medium sweet wine and three for a sweet wine. The saccharin, which is not fermentable, cannot be tasted, and the wine can subsequently be kept for as long as you wish. If sugar or a syrup is preferred, the wine should be served almost as soon as it is sweetened in case any living yeast cells remain in the wine and start a further fermentation.

Sparkling wines are sometimes underrated by the amateur who is put off by the priming fermentation and the removal of the secondary sediment. The whole operation, in fact, takes only a few seconds if it is properly organized beforehand. The little extra effort certainly pays dividends with the superb wine which results.

AVOIDING AND SOLVING PROBLEMS

Most problems can be avoided in winemaking by strict attention to hygiene, the use of good ingredients and pure wine yeasts, the addition of sufficient acid and nutrient, keeping the must and wine covered at all times, racking promptly at the end of fermentation, keeping jars full and wise use of Campden tablets. Even so, very occasionally, something can go wrong.

The most common problems are as follows:

1) **Stuck ferments.** See page 19.
2) **Haze in the finished wine.** This may be due to pectin from fruit, starch from vegetables or to suspended solids. A metal haze is unlikely since no metallic equipment should ever be used other than high grade stainless steel.

Pectin: Test for this haze by mixing 15 ml/1 tablespoon of the finished wine in 45 ml/3 tablespoons of methylated spirits. Pour the mixture into a small bottle, shake well and leave it for an hour. If strings or dots appear in the liquid, the cause of the haze is pectin. Mix a pectin-destroying enzyme into the wine (10 ml/2 teaspoons per 5 litres/1 gallon), leave it in a warm place for 48 hours and then move it to a cool place for a few days while the sediment settles. Rack, add one Campden tablet and store.

Starch: Test for this haze by mixing a few drops of household iodine into 15 ml/1 tablespoon of the wine. If the colour darkens or turns blue, the cause of the haze is starch. Mix into the wine some fungal amylase in the proportion recommended by the manufacturer. Stir well and leave first in a warm place for 48 hours and then in a cool place until the wine is bright. Rack, add one Campden tablet and store.

Suspended particles: Stir in a proprietary brand of wine finings made from either bentonite, isinglass or kieselguhr. Shake well, then leave the wine in a cool place to clear. Rack, add one Campden tablet and store.

Note A few 15 ml spoons/tablespoons of fresh milk frequently clear a hazy apple wine. The white of one egg beaten up in some wine is enough to fine 25 litres/5 gallons of wine.

3) **Off smells and flavours.** This is any smell or flavour that is not clean and attractive. It is probably caused by an imperfectly sterilized piece of equipment or a stale, infected ingredient. There is rarely anything that can be done to help such a wine. If the smell and flavour are too bad, the wine should be thrown away, the container washed in hot water and sterilized.

4) **Vinegary smell or taste.** This is probably due to using infected fruit, leaving the must or wine uncovered, racking the wine in a room where chutney or spiced vinegar was being boiled or the use of a poor or infected yeast. If the smell is only slight, two crushed Campden tablets might correct the fault, but the wine will, most likely, have to be discarded and the equipment thoroughly washed and sterilized.

5) **Rotting vegetable smell.** This occurs if the wine has been left on its lees after fermentation has finished. There is no remedy. The wine should be discarded, and the vessel washed and sterilized.

6) **Bad egg smell.** Certain yeasts can produce hydrogen sulphide, the cause of this smell, when there is insufficient acid and nutrient in the wine during fermentation. There is no remedy. Ensure that you always include sufficient acid and nutrient in the future.

7) **Flat, brown taste.** This is due to oxidation and is caused by using bruised or damaged fruit, by leaving the must insufficiently covered or protected by sulphite, by failing to include one Campden tablet per 5 litres/1 gallon at the first racking or by leaving a jar or cask of low alcohol/low acid wine insufficiently full.

Sometimes the oxidation can be remedied by a re-fermentation, but this is not always easy to start. The best way is to make up 500 ml/17 fl oz of an activated yeast in a starter bottle, and to add 500 ml/17 fl oz of the wine and 5 ml/1 teaspoon of sugar. When it is fermenting, add 1 litre/2 pints of wine and 10 ml/2 teaspoons of sugar, and so on. Always add the oxidized wine to the fermenting wine in equal proportions. When fermentation is finished, rack and add one Campden tablet per 5 litres/1 gallon wine, then treat as a new wine.

A fermentation that has temporarily stopped can also be restarted as a last resort in this way.

8) **Ropiness.** The wine develops a shine, looks thick and pours like a thin oil. This is due to lactic acid bacteria that form ropes in the wine; it can be remedied as follows: beat the wine well with a wooden spoon to break up the ropes, add two crushed Campden tablets per 5 litres/1 gallon wine, then bung tight and leave in a cool place for two or three days until a deposit has formed and the wine looks normal. Rack the wine from the deposit into a sterilized jar.

9) **Mousiness.** A wine low in acid can develop a smell and taste reminiscent of mice. This is due to a fungus infection and if the smell and taste is bad, the wine should be discarded and the container washed and sterilized.

10) **Pear drop smell.** This is caused by yeast short of nutrient. There is no remedy. If the wine is undrinkable, it should be discarded, bearing in mind that sufficient nutrient should be included the next time.

11) **Bitter almond smell.** If fruit stones or pips are included in the fermenting must, there will be a bitter almond smell. There is no remedy. If the wine is undrinkable, it should be discarded.

12) **No bouquet and a medicinal taste.** This is caused by a lack of acid in the fermenting wine. There are two ways of improving this. The first is to blend the finished wine with one that contains too much acid, and the second is to add the wine to a fermenting must and to include an extra 15 ml/1 tablespoon of citric acid.

13) **Malo-lactic ferment.** This is not strictly an ailment. If a wine containing malic acid, eg made from apples, apricots, blackberries, cherries, damsons, gooseberries, greengages, loganberries, peaches or rhubarb is not sulphited after racking, one of the lactic acid bacteria may convert the malic acid to lactic acid. This softens the taste of the wine since lactic acid is not as sharp tasting as malic acid. A small quantity of carbon dioxide is produced, however, and may be enough to blow a cork or even burst a jar or bottle.

The different stages of fermentation demonstrate very clearly how wine develops from a cloudy unrecognizable liquid to one which is crystal clear and bright.

RECIPES

The recipes which follow are only a sample of the wide range available to you. They can, however, be described as the best of home-made wines. They have been made many times and have always proved enjoyable. Each recipe makes 6 × 75 cl/26 oz bottles of wine.

If in any doubt about any of the procedures mentioned in the recipes, refer back to the detailed instructions on pages 17–26.

Note When making table wines, you may substitute 250 g/ 8 oz concentrated grape juice, 1 kg/2 lb fresh grapes or 600 ml/20 oz bottled grape juice for 250 g/8 oz sultanas or raisins. Double the quantity can be used for dessert wines.

If the wine tastes too dry for your palate, add 1–2 saccharin pellets to each bottle of wine. The improvement is quite remarkable.

APPLE TABLE WINE

4.5 kg/9 lb unpeeled apples of mixed varieties, washed and chopped
2 litres/4 pints cold water
5 ml/1 tsp citric acid
5 ml/1 tsp pectic enzyme
250 g/8 oz sultanas, washed and chopped
2 Campden tablets
2.5 ml/½ tsp grape tannin
activated Champagne wine yeast
2.5 ml/½ tsp nutrient
875 g/1¾ lb white sugar

1) Drop the apples into a bin containing the water, acid, pectic enzyme, sultanas and 1 crushed Campden tablet. Cover and leave in a warm place for 24 hours while the enzyme works.
2) Stir in the tannin, yeast and nutrient, and ferment on the pulp for 6 days, keeping the fruit submerged and the bin covered.
3) Strain out, press dry and discard the fruit, stir in the sugar, pour the must into a fermentation jar, top up if necessary, fit an airlock and ferment out.
4) Siphon the clearing wine into a sterilized storage jar, top up, add 1 Campden tablet, bung tight, label and store in a cold place until the wine is bright.
5) Rack again, mature for 1 year in bulk, then bottle.

VARIATIONS

The addition of 1 kg/2 lb bitter-sweet crabapples and another 500 g/1 lb sugar will make a richer, sweeter wine.

APPLE SPARKLING WINE

4.5 kg/9 lb unpeeled apples of mixed varieties, washed
  and chopped
2 litres/4 pints cold water
5 ml/1 tsp citric acid
5 ml/1 tsp pectic enzyme
250 g/8 oz sultanas, washed and chopped
2 Campden tablets
2.5 ml/½ tsp grape tannin
activated Champagne wine yeast
2.5 ml/½ tsp nutrient
875 g/1¾ lb white sugar
75 g/2½ oz caster sugar
additional activated Champagne wine yeast

1) Drop the apples into a bin containing the water, acid, pectic enzyme, sultanas and 1 crushed Campden tablet. Cover and leave in a warm place for 24 hours while the enzyme works.
2) Stir in the tannin, yeast and nutrient, and ferment on the pulp for 6 days, keeping the fruit submerged and the bin covered.
3) Strain out, press dry and discard the fruit, stir in the white sugar, pour the must into a fermentation jar, top up if necessary, fit an airlock and ferment out.
4) Siphon the wine into a sterilized storage jar, top up, add 1 Campden tablet, bung tight, label and store in a cold place until the wine is bright. This will take 6 months.
5) Mix in the caster sugar, additional Champagne wine yeast and pinch of nutrient into the jar, fit an airlock and leave in a warm place for a few hours.
6) As soon as fermentation starts, siphon the wine into sterilized champagne bottles.
7) Fit softened, hollow-doomed or blister stoppers, wire them on and leave the bottles on their sides for at least 6 months before disgorging the secondary sediment.
8) When disgorging, add 1 or 2 saccharin pellets before fitting a clean stopper.

APPLE AND BLACKBERRY TABLE WINE

4.5 kg/9 lb unpeeled cooking and eating apples, washed
  and chopped
2 litres/4 pints cold water
5 ml/1 tsp citric acid
5 ml/1 tsp pectic enzyme
1 kg/2 lb blackberries, hulled, washed and crushed
250 g/8 oz sultanas, washed and chopped
2 Campden tablets
2.5 ml/½ tsp grape tannin
activated Bordeaux wine yeast
2.5 ml/½ tsp nutrient
875 g/1¾ lb white sugar

1) Drop the apples into a bin containing the water, acid, pectic enzyme, the blackberries, sultanas and 1 crushed Campden tablet. Cover and leave in a warm place for 24 hours while the enzyme works.
2) Stir in the tannin, yeast and nutrient, and ferment on the pulp for 6 days, keeping the fruit submerged and the bin covered.
3) Strain out, press dry and discard the fruit, stir in the sugar, pour the must into a fermentation jar, top up if necessary, fit an airlock and ferment out.
4) Siphon the clearing wine into a sterilized storage jar, top up, add 1 Campden tablet, bung tight, label and store in a cold place until the wine is bright.
5) Rack again and mature this dry, light red wine for 1 year in bulk, then bottle. Serve it with cold meats and picnics.

VARIATION

Apple and Raspberry Wine
Substitute 500 g/1 lb raspberries for the blackberries.

APPLE AND ELDERBERRY TABLE WINE

4.5 kg/9 lb unpeeled cooking and eating apples, washed
    and chopped
2 litres/4 pints cold water
5 ml/1 tsp citric acid
5 ml/1 tsp pectic enzyme
500 g/1 lb elderberries, stalked, washed and crushed
250 g/8 oz raisins, washed and chopped
2 Campden tablets
activated Bordeaux wine yeast
2.5 ml/½ tsp nutrient
875 g/1¾ lb white sugar

1) Drop the apples into a bin containing the water, acid, pectic enzyme, elderberries, raisins and 1 crushed Campden tablet. Cover and leave in a warm place for 24 hours while the enzyme works.
2) Stir in the yeast and nutrient, and ferment on the pulp for 6 days, keeping the fruit submerged and the bin covered.
3) Strain out, press dry and discard the fruit, stir in the sugar, pour the must into a fermentation jar, top up if necessary, fit an airlock and ferment out.
4) Siphon the clearing wine into a storage jar, top up, add 1 Campden tablet, bung tight, label and store in a cool place until the wine is bright.
5) Rack again and mature this dry, light red wine for at least 1 year in bulk, then bottle and keep it for at least another 6 months. Serve it free from chill with lamb cutlets, stuffed breast of lamb, etc.

Note No tannin is required for this wine.

APRICOT TABLE WINE

2.25 kg/4½ lb fresh apricots, washed, stoned and chopped
250 g/8 oz sultanas, washed and chopped
3.75 litres/7½ pints cold water
5 ml/1 tsp citric acid
5 ml/1 tsp pectic enzyme
2 Campden tablets
2.5 ml/½ tsp grape tannin
activated Chablis wine yeast
2.5 ml/½ tsp nutrient
1 kg/2 lb white sugar

1) Put the pieces of apricot and sultana into a bin containing the water, acid, pectic enzyme and 1 crushed Campden tablet. Cover and leave in a warm place for 24 hours while the enzyme works.
2) Add the tannin, yeast and nutrient, and ferment on the pulp for 4 days, keeping the fruit submerged and the bin covered.
3) Strain out, press dry and discard the fruit, stir in the sugar, pour the must into a fermentation jar, top up if necessary, fit an airlock and ferment out.
4) Siphon the clearing wine into a storage jar, top up, add 1 Campden tablet, bung tight, label and store in a cold place until the wine is bright.
5) Rack again and mature for 1 year before bottling. Serve as a dry white table wine.

DRIED APRICOT TABLE WINE

375 g/12 oz dried apricots, washed and chopped
3.75 litres/7½ pints hot water
500 g/1 lb sultanas, washed and chopped
5 ml/1 tsp citric acid
5 ml/1 tsp pectic enzyme
2 Campden tablets
2.5 ml/½ tsp grape tannin
activated Chablis wine yeast
2.5 ml/½ tsp nutrient
1 kg/2 lb white sugar

1) Put the fruit in a bin, pour on the hot water, cover and leave overnight to cool.
2) Add the sultanas, stir in the acid, enzyme and 1 crushed Campden tablet, cover and leave in a warm place for 24 hours.
3) Add the tannin, yeast and nutrient, and ferment on the pulp for 4 days, keeping the fruit submerged and the bin covered.
4) Strain out, press dry and discard the fruit, stir in the sugar, pour the must into a fermentation jar, top up if necessary, fit an airlock and ferment out.
5) Siphon the clearing wine into a storage jar, top up, add 1 Campden tablet, bung tight, label and store in a cold place until the wine is bright.
6) Rack again and mature for 1 year before bottling.

BEETROOT DESSERT WINE

2.25 kg/4½ lb young beetroot, topped, tailed, scrubbed
   clean and thinly sliced
3 litres/6 pints cold water
500 g/1 lb concentrated red grape juice
10 ml/2 tsps citric acid
5 ml/1 tsp grape tannin
activated port wine yeast
5 ml/1 tsp nutrient
1.5 kg/3 lb white sugar

1) Boil the beetroot in the water in a covered pan for
    1 hour until tender. Leave to cool.
2) Strain the liquor into a fermentation jar, add the
    concentrated grape juice, acid, tannin, yeast and
    nutrient. Leave room for the sugar, fit an airlock and
    ferment at around 21°C/70°F.
3) After 5 days, remove some of the must, stir in one-
    third of the sugar and return it to the jar. Replace the
    airlock and continue the fermentation for 7 days.
4) Repeat the process with half the remaining sugar, re-fit
    the airlock and ferment for another 7 days.
5) Add the last of the sugar, top up if necessary, then
    ferment out.
6) Siphon the clearing wine into a storage jar, top up,
    bung tight, label and store in a cool place until the
    wine is bright.
7) Rack again and mature this wine in bulk for 2 years
    before bottling. Serve it free from chill, either as a
    sweet dessert wine after a meal or with cheese and
    biscuits.

Note Neither pectic enzyme nor a Campden tablet is
necessary.

CARROT DESSERT WINE

2.5 kg/4½ lb carrots, topped, tailed, scrubbed clean and
   thinly sliced
3 litres/6 pints cold water
500 g/1 lb concentrated white grape juice
10 ml/2 tsps citric acid
5 ml/1 tsp grape tannin
activated Tokay wine yeast
5 ml/1 tsp nutrient
1.5 kg/3 lb white sugar

1) Boil the carrots in the water in a covered pan for 1
    hour until tender. Leave to cool.
2) Strain the liquor into a fermentation jar, add the
    concentrated grape juice, acid, tannin, yeast and
    nutrient. Leave room for the sugar, fit an airlock and
    ferment at around 21°C/70°F.
3) After 5 days, remove some of the must, stir in one-
    third of the sugar, and return it to the jar. Replace the
    airlock and continue the fermentation for 7 days.
4) Repeat the process with half the remaining sugar, re-fit
    the airlock and ferment for another 7 days.
5) Add the last of the sugar, top up if necessary, then
    ferment out.
6) Siphon the clearing wine into a storage jar, top up,
    bung tight, label and store in a cool place until the
    wine is bright.
7) Rack again and mature this wine in bulk for 2 years
    before bottling. Serve as for Beetroot Dessert Wine.

Note Neither pectic enzyme nor a Campden tablet is
necessary.

PARSNIP AND FIG DESSERT WINE

2.25 kg/4½ lb fresh parsnips, topped, tailed, scrubbed
  clean and diced
4 litres/8 pints water
175 g/6 oz dried figs, washed and chopped
500 g/1 lb muscatel raisins, washed and chopped
15 ml/1 tbsp citric acid
2.5 ml/½ tsp grape tannin
activated Madeira wine yeast
2.5 ml/½ tsp nutrient
1.5 kg/3 lb light brown sugar

1) Boil the parsnips in the water in a covered pan until soft and tender but not mushy.
2) Strain the hot liquor into a bin containing the chopped figs and muscatels, the acid and the tannin. Stir well, cover and leave to cool.
3) Stir in the yeast and nutrient, and ferment on the pulp for 5 days, keeping the pulp submerged and the bin covered.
4) Strain out, press dry and discard the pulp. Stir in half the sugar, pour the must into a fermentation jar, leave room for the rest of the sugar, fit an airlock and ferment for 10 days.
5) Repeat with half the remaining sugar, re-fit the airlock and continue fermentation for another 10 days.
6) Repeat this process with the last of the sugar and ferment out.
7) Siphon the clearing wine into a storage jar, top up, bung tight, label and keep in a cool place until the wine is bright.
8) Rack again, sweeten to taste if necessary with brown sugar, and then store in a warm place for 6 months. Mature for another year before bottling. This wine should finish strong and sweet with a distinctive caramel flavour.

Note No enzyme or Campden tablets are needed for this wine.

BILBERRY TABLE WINE

1 kg/2 lb bottled bilberries in syrup
500 g/1 lb blackberries in syrup
3 litres/6 pints cold water
10 ml/2 tsps citric acid
5 ml/1 tsp pectic enzyme
2 Campden tablets
250 g/8 oz concentrated red grape juice
2.5 ml/½ tsp grape tannin
activated Bordeaux wine yeast
2.5 ml/½ tsp nutrient
1 kg/2 lb white sugar

1) Strain off the syrup from the fruit into a sterilized bottle and store in a refrigerator for later use.
2) Mash the fruit in a bin, pour on the cold water and stir in the acid, enzyme and 1 crushed Campden tablet. Cover and leave for 24 hours while the enzyme works.
3) Stir in the grape juice, reserved syrup, tannin, yeast and nutrient, and ferment on the pulp for 3 days, keeping the fruit submerged and the bin covered.
4) Strain out, press dry and discard the fruit, stir in the sugar, pour the must into a fermentation jar, top up, fit an airlock and ferment out.
5) Siphon the wine into a storage jar, top up, add 1 Campden tablet, bung tight, label and store until it is bright.
6) Rack again, mature in bulk for 6 months, then bottle and store for a further 3 months. Serve free from chill as a dry red table wine with roast meats.

BLACKBERRY TABLE WINE

2.25 kg/4½ lb blackberries, hulled, washed and crushed
3 litres/6 pints hot water
5 ml/1 tsp citric acid
5 ml/1 tsp pectic enzyme
2 Campden tablets
250 g/8 oz concentrated red grape juice
5 ml/1 tsp grape tannin
activated Bordeaux wine yeast
2.5 ml/½ tsp nutrient
1 kg/2 lb white sugar

1) Place the blackberries in a bin, pour on the hot water, cover and leave to cool.
2) Stir in the acid, enzyme and 1 crushed Campden tablet, replace the cover and leave for 24 hours.
3) Stir in the grape juice, tannin, yeast and nutrient, and ferment on the pulp for 3 days, keeping the fruit submerged and the bin covered.
4) Strain out, press dry and discard the fruit, stir in the sugar, pour the must into a fermentation jar, top up if necessary, fit an airlock and ferment out.
5) Siphon the clearing wine into a storage jar, top up, add 1 Campden tablet, bung tight, label and store in a cool place until the wine is clear.
6) Rack again and mature this dry red wine in bulk for at least 1 year before bottling. Serve it free from chill with roast meats.

BLACKBERRY DESSERT WINE

2.25 kg/4½ lb blackberries, hulled, washed and crushed
2 very ripe bananas, peeled and mashed
250 g/8 oz raisins, washed and chopped
250 g/8 oz prunes, washed, stoned and chopped
3.75 litres/7½ pints hot water
10 ml/2 tsps citric acid
5 ml/1 tsp pectic enzyme
1 Campden tablet
activated port wine yeast
5 ml/1 tsp nutrient
1 kg/2 lb white sugar

1) Place the fruit in a bin, pour hot water over it, cover and leave to cool.
2) Stir in the acid, pectic enzyme and crushed Campden tablet, replace the cover and leave in a warm place for 24 hours.
3) Stir in the yeast and nutrient, then ferment on the pulp for 4 days, keeping the fruit submerged and the bin covered.
4) Strain out, press dry and discard the pulp. Stir in one-third of the sugar, pour the must into a fermentation jar, leave room for the rest of the sugar, fit an airlock, then ferment for 7 days.
5) Repeat this process with half the remaining sugar, re-fit the airlock and ferment for another 7 days.
6) Repeat this process with the last of the sugar, top up if necessary and ferment out.
7) Siphon the clearing wine into a storage jar, top up, bung tight, label and keep in a cool place until the wine is bright.
8) Rack again and keep for 2 years in bulk, then bottle.

DAMSON TABLE WINE

2.25 kg/4½ lb ripe damsons, stalked, washed, stoned
  and crushed
250 g/8 oz raisins, washed and chopped
4 litres/8 pints hot water
5 ml/1 tsp citric acid
5 ml/1 tsp pectic enzyme
2 Campden tablets
activated Burgundy wine yeast
2.5 ml/½ tsp nutrient
1 kg/2 lb white sugar

1) Place the damsons and raisins in a bin, pour on the hot water, cover and leave to cool.
2) Stir in the citric acid, pectic enzyme and 1 crushed Campden tablet, replace the cover and leave for 24 hours.
3) Stir in the yeast and nutrient, and ferment on the pulp for 5 days, keeping the fruit submerged and the bin covered.
4) Strain out, press dry and discard the fruit, stir in the sugar, pour the must into a fermentation jar, top up if necessary, fit an airlock and ferment out.
5) Siphon the clearing wine into a storage jar, top up, add 1 Campden tablet, bung tight, label and store in a cool place until the wine is bright.
6) Rack again and mature in bulk for at least 1 year before bottling. Serve as a dry red table wine.

Note No tannin is required for this recipe.

VARIATION

Black Plum Table Wine
Substitute 2.25 kg/4½ lb black plums for the damsons, and make as above.

DAMSON DESSERT WINE

2.75 kg/5½ lb ripe damsons, stalked, washed, stoned
  and crushed
500 g/1 lb raisins, washed and chopped
250 g/8 oz prunes, washed, stoned and chopped
3.3 litres/6½ pints hot water
5 ml/1 tsp citric acid
5 ml/1 tsp pectic enzyme
1 Campden tablet
2.5 ml/½ tsp grape tannin
activated port wine yeast
5 ml/1 tsp nutrient
1.5 kg/3 lb white sugar

1) Place the damsons, raisins, and prunes in a bin and pour hot water over them, cover and leave to cool.
2) Stir in the acid, enzyme and 1 crushed Campden tablet, replace the cover and leave in a warm place for 24 hours.
3) Stir in the tannin, yeast and nutrient, and ferment on the pulp for 5 days, keeping the fruit submerged and the bin covered.
4) Strain out, press dry and discard the fruit, stir in half the sugar, pour the must into a fermentation jar, leave room for the rest of the sugar, fit an airlock and ferment for 10 days.
5) Repeat this process with half the remaining sugar, re-fit the airlock and continue the fermentation for another 10 days.
6) Repeat again with the last of the sugar, top up if necessary and ferment out.
7) Siphon the clearing wine into a storage jar, top up, bung tight, label and keep in a cool place until the wine is bright.
8) Rack again and keep for 2 years in bulk, then bottle and keep for a further 6 months. Serve this strong, sweet, dessert wine after dinner with Stilton cheese.

DANDELION WINE

2 litres/3¼ pints dandelion heads
3.75 litres/7½ pints hot water
2 Campden tablets
1 kg/2 lb concentrated white grape juice
activated Sauternes wine yeast
300 g/10 oz white sugar

1) Gather the flowers on a dry sunny day, discard the green seed boxes, stems and leaves, empty the petals into a bin, pour hot water over them, then rub them against the side of the bin with the back of a wooden spoon to squeeze out the fragrant essence. Cover and leave to cool, then add 1 crushed Campden tablet.

2) Repeat this maceration of the petals twice more on the following day, then strain out, press dry and discard the petals.

3) Stir the concentrated grape juice and activated yeast into the liquor, pour the must into a fermentation jar, leave room for the sugar, fit an airlock and ferment for 10 days in a warm place.

4) Remove some of the must, stir in the sugar, return it to the jar, re-fit the airlock and ferment out.

5) Siphon the clearing wine into a storage jar, top up, add 1 Campden tablet, bung tight, label and store in a cool place until the wine is bright.

6) Rack into bottles, sweetening the wine to taste with saccharin, and store for 6 months. Serve this wine cold, as a social wine with sweet biscuits.

Note No acid, enzyme or tannin is required.
Remember that bulbous and tuberous flowers are *poisonous*, so should *not* be used.

VARIATIONS

Elderflower Wine
Substitute 600 ml/1 pint elderflower florets for the dandelion heads.
Rose Wine
Substitute 2 litres/3¼ pints of fragrant rose petals.

DATE AND RHUBARB WINE

1 kg/2 lb loose dates, stoned and chopped
1 kg/2 lb rhubarb, topped, tailed, washed and
   chopped small
500 g/1 lb raisins, washed and chopped
thinly pared rind and juice of 1 large orange
4.4 litres/9 pints cold water
10 ml/2 tsps citric acid
5 ml/1 tsp pectic enzyme
1 Campden tablet
2.5 ml/½ tsp grape tannin
activated sherry flor wine yeast
2.5 ml/½ tsp nutrient
1 kg/2 lb white sugar

1) Place the dates, rhubarb, raisins, orange rind and juice in a bin containing the water, acid, enzyme and 1 crushed Campden tablet. Cover and leave for 24 hours.
2) Stir in the tannin, yeast and nutrient, and ferment on the pulp for 6 days, keeping the fruit submerged and the bin covered.
3) Strain out, press dry and discard the pulp, stir in one-third of the sugar, and pour the must into a fermentation jar. Plug the neck with cotton wool instead of an airlock and ferment for 10 days.
4) Remove some of the must, stir in another third of the sugar, return the must to the jar, replace the cotton wool and leave for another 10 days.
5) Repeat this process with the last portion of sugar and ferment out.
6) Siphon the young wine from its sediment into a storage jar, leaving an air gap in the jar. Plug the neck with cotton wool again, label and store in a cool place until the wine is bright.
7) Rack again, thereby increasing the air gap slightly. Replace the cotton wool and mature for 18 months in bulk before bottling. Serve this sherry-style wine cool, as an apéritif, or blend it with another sherry-style wine after 12 months in bulk storage.

ELDERBERRY TABLE WINE

1 kg/2 lb elderberries, stalked, washed and crushed
250 g/8 oz raisins, washed and chopped
2 very ripe bananas, peeled and mashed
4.4 litres/9 pints hot water
10 ml/2 tsps citric acid
5 ml/1 tsp pectic enzyme
2 Campden tablets
activated Bordeaux wine yeast
2.5 ml/½ tsp nutrient
1 kg/2 lb white sugar

1) Place the fruit in a bin, pour hot water over it, cover and leave to cool.
2) Add the acid, pectic enzyme and 1 crushed Campden tablet, replace the cover and leave for 24 hours.
3) Stir in the yeast and nutrient, and ferment on the pulp for 6 days keeping the fruit submerged and the bin covered.
4) Strain out, press dry and discard the fruit, stir in the sugar, pour the must into a fermentation jar, top up if necessary, fit an airlock and ferment out.
5) Siphon the clearing wine into a storage jar, top up, add 1 Campden tablet, bung tight, label and store until the wine is bright.
6) Rack again and store in bulk until the wine is at least 1 year old before bottling. It improves with further storage. Serve free from chill as a red table wine.

Note Since the elderberry flavour is very strong, the wine should be sweetened if more elderberries than the quantity recommended are used.

ELDERBERRY DESSERT WINE

1 kg/2 lb elderberries, stalked, washed and crushed
1 kg/2 lb bottled bilberries in syrup
1 kg/2 lb damsons, stalked, washed, stoned and crushed
250 g/8 oz raisins, washed and chopped
3 litres/6 pints hot water
10 ml/2 tsps citric acid
5 ml/1 tsp pectic enzyme
1 Campden tablet
activated port wine yeast
2.5 ml/½ tsp nutrient
1.5 kg/3 lb white sugar

1) Place all the fruit in a bin, pour hot water over it, cover and leave to cool.
2) Stir in the acid, enzyme and 1 crushed Campden tablet, replace the cover and leave for 24 hours.
3) Stir in the yeast and nutrient, and ferment on the pulp for 6 days, keeping the fruit submerged and the bin covered.
4) Strain out, press dry and discard the pulp, stir in half the sugar, pour the must into a fermentation jar, leave room for the rest of the sugar, fit an airlock and ferment for 10 days.
5) Remove some of the must, stir in half the remaining sugar, return the must to the jar, re-fit the airlock and continue the fermentation for another 10 days.
6) Repeat this process with the last of the sugar, top up if necessary and ferment out.
7) Siphon the clearing wine into a storage jar, top up, bung tight, label and store in a cool place until the wine is bright.
8) Rack again, then mature this strong, sweet, dessert wine in bulk for 2 years before bottling. Keep for as long as you can in bottles. Serve it after a meal with cheese.

Note No tannin is required for this recipe.

FIG AND ROSE-HIP WINE

175 g/6 oz dried figs, washed and chopped
275 g/9 oz rose-hip shells, washed and chopped
275 g/9 oz raisins, washed and chopped
4 litres/8 pints hot water
15 ml/1 tbsp citric acid
5 ml/1 tsp pectic enzyme
1 Campden tablet
2.5 ml/½ tsp grape tannin
activated sherry flor wine yeast
2.5 ml/½ tsp nutrient
1.5 kg/3 lb white sugar

1) Place the figs, rose-hips and raisins in a bin and pour hot water over them. Cover and leave to cool.
2) Add the acid, enzyme and 1 crushed Campden tablet, cover and leave for 24 hours.
3) Stir in the tannin, yeast and nutrient, and ferment on the pulp for 5 days, keeping the fruit submerged and the bin covered.
4) Strain out, press dry and discard the pulp, stir in half the sugar, and pour the must into a fermentation jar. Plug the neck with cotton wool instead of an airlock and ferment for 10 days.
5) Remove some of the must, stir in half the remaining sugar, return the must to the jar, replace the cotton wool and leave for another 10 days.
6) Repeat this process with the remaining sugar and ferment out.
7) Siphon the clearing wine into a storage jar, leaving an air gap in the jar. Plug the neck with cotton wool again, label and store in a cool place until the wine is bright.
8) Rack again, thereby increasing the air gap slightly. Replace the cotton wool and mature for at least 1 year in bulk before bottling. Serve this wine cold, as a dry apéritif, or blend with a similar wine after storing in bulk for 12 months.

Note Dried rose-hip shells are available from home-brew centres and suppliers.

FOLLY

After vines have flowered in June, surplus shoots should be pruned. These can be made into an attractive dry table wine.

3 kg/6 lb vine prunings, washed and chopped small
3.75 litres/7½ pints hot water
250 g/8 oz concentrated white grape juice
10 ml/2 tsps citric acid
activated German wine yeast
2.5 ml/½ tsp nutrient
1 kg/2 lb white sugar
1 Campden tablet

1) Place the prunings in a bin, pour on the hot water, cover and leave to cool.
2) Stir in the concentrated grape juice, the acid, yeast and nutrient. Ferment on the pulp for 5 days, keeping the leaves submerged and the bin covered.
3) Strain out, press dry and discard the pulp, stir in the sugar, pour the must into a fermentation jar, top up if necessary, fit an airlock and ferment out.
4) Siphon into a storage jar, top up, add 1 Campden tablet, bung tight, label and store until the wine is bright.
5) Rack again and mature the wine in bulk for 1 year before bottling.

Note Pectic enzyme is not required.

VARIATION

Bramble shoots may be used in a similar way.

GOOSEBERRY SPARKLING WINE

1.5 kg/3 lb just ripe gooseberries, topped, tailed and washed
250 g/8 oz sultanas, washed and chopped
4.4 litres/9 pints hot water
5 ml/1 tsp citric acid
5 ml/1 tsp pectic enzyme
1 Campden tablet
activated Champagne wine yeast
2.5 ml/½ tsp nutrient
875 g/1¾ lb white sugar
75 g/2½ oz caster sugar
additional activated Champagne wine yeast

1) Place the fruit in a bin, pour on the hot water, cover and leave to cool, then crush the berries.
2) Stir in the acid, pectic enzyme and 1 crushed Campden tablet, replace the cover and leave for 24 hours.
3) Stir in the activated yeast and 2.5 ml/½ tsp nutrient, and ferment on the pulp for 3 days, keeping the fruit submerged and the bin covered.
4) Strain out, press dry and discard the fruit, stir in the white sugar, pour the must into a fermentation jar, top up if necessary, fit an airlock and ferment out.
5) Siphon the clearing wine into a storage jar, top up, bung tight, label and store until the wine is bright.
6) When the wine is crystal clear and 6 months old, mix the caster sugar, additional Champagne yeast and a pinch of nutrient into the jar, fit an airlock and leave in a warm place for a few hours.
7) As soon as fermentation starts, siphon the wine into sterilized champagne bottles.
8) Fit softened, hollow-domed or blister stoppers, wire them on and leave the bottles on their sides for at least 6 months before disgorging the secondary sediment.
9) At the time of disgorgement, add 1 or 2 saccharin pellets before fitting a clean stopper.

GOOSEBERRY DESSERT WINE

2.25 kg/4½ lb golden ripe gooseberries, topped, tailed, washed and crushed
500 g/1 lb sultanas, washed and chopped
4 litres/8 pints cold water
10 ml/2 tsps citric acid
5 ml/1 tsp pectic enzyme
1 Campden tablet
2.5 ml/½ tsp grape tannin
activated Sauternes wine yeast
2.5 ml/½ tsp nutrient
1 kg/2 lb white sugar

1) Place the gooseberries and sultanas in a bin containing the water, acid, enzyme and 1 crushed Campden tablet. Cover and leave in a warm place for 24 hours while the enzyme works.
2) Stir in the tannin, yeast and nutrient, and ferment on the pulp for 5 days, keeping the fruit submerged and the bin covered.
3) Strain out, press dry and discard the fruit, stir in half the sugar, and pour the must into a fermentation jar, leaving room for the rest of the sugar. Fit an airlock and ferment for 10 days in a warm place.
4) Remove some of the must, stir in the rest of the sugar, return the must to the jar, re-fit the airlock and ferment out.
5) Siphon the clearing wine into a storage jar, top up, bung tight, label and leave in a cool place until the wine is bright.
6) Rack again and, if necessary sweeten to taste with saccharin. 15 ml/1 tablespoonful of glycerine is an optional extra to add smoothness and richness to the wine. Store in bulk for 1 year, then bottle and serve this wine cold with the dessert course of a meal.

GRAPE WINES

DRY WHITE

Several varieties suitable for making into wine are now grown in Britain, eg Seyve-Villard and Müller-Thurgau. Wine can also be made from the sultana grapes imported in August. Even better wine is made by mixing together the grapes from different varieties.

To make 5 litres/5 quarts of wine you need:

9 kg/18 lb white grapes, stalked, washed and crushed
5 ml/1 tsp pectic enzyme
2 Campden tablets
sugar as necessary
activated Hock yeast

1) Place the grapes in a bin, add pectic enzyme and 1 crushed Campden tablet, cover and leave in a warm place for 24 hours.
2) Strain out, press dry and discard the skins and pips, measure the specific gravity of the must and stir in sufficient sugar to bring the reading up to SG 1.080 or just below.
3) Add the yeast, pour the must into a fermentation jar, fit an airlock and ferment out in a cool temperature.
4) Siphon the young wine into a storage jar, top up with white wine, add 1 Campden tablet, bung tight, label and store in a cool place until the wine is bright.
5) Rack into bottles and mature this white table wine for 1 year. Serve it cold.

Note The grapes contain sufficient acid, tannin, nutrient and water.

This wine is best matured in bottles rather than in a jar if you wish to capture the grapey flavour.

MEDIUM SWEET WHITE

This can be made by adding some bought Almeria or Muscatel grapes to home-grown grapes. A ratio of one measure of bought grapes to four measures of your own is about right.

1) Prepare the must as for dry white wine.
2) Measure the specific gravity, and, if necessary, increase it to about 1.086.
3) Ferment the must with an activated Sauternes yeast. When the specific gravity drops to 1.008, stir in a proprietary brand of wine finings as directed by the manufacturer, together with 1.25 ml/¼ tsp potassium sorbate and 1 Campden tablet per 5 litres/1 gallon of must.
4) Leave in as cold a place as possible for a few days while the wine clears, then siphon it into a storage jar, adding another Campden tablet per 5 litres/1 gallon of wine. Top up, bung tight, label and store in a cool place for 1 month.
5) Rack into bottles and mature for another 3–9 months. Serve cold at any time.

Note The Almeria, and the Muscatel grapes, even more so, impart a very attractive flavour to the wine.

GRAPE WINES

RED

Seibel and Bacco are the popular outdoor grape varieties and make an interesting wine when mixed with some imported Italian black grapes.

9 kg/18 lb black grapes, stalked, washed and crushed
5 ml/1 tsp pectic enzyme
2 Campden tablets
sugar as necessary
activated Burgundy wine yeast

1) Place the grapes in a bin, add the pectic enzyme and 1 crushed Campden tablet, cover and leave in a warm place for 24 hours.
2) Strain out some juice, check the specific gravity and increase the reading to 1.090 with white sugar.
3) Add the yeast and ferment on the pulp for 10 days, keeping the skins submerged and the bin covered.
4) Strain out, press dry and discard the skins and pips, pour the must into a fermentation jar, fit an airlock and ferment out.
5) Siphon into a storage jar, top up with red wine, add 1 Campden tablet, bung tight, label and store until the wine is bright.
6) Rack again and store in a jar for 2 years before bottling. Serve it free from chill as a table wine.

ROSÉ

This can be made from a mixture of white and black grapes.

1) Prepare and ferment as for red wine, increasing the specific gravity to 1.080. When the juice has attained a pretty pink colour, usually within 24 hours or so, strain out, press dry and discard the skins and pips.
2) Pour the must into a fermentation jar, fit an airlock and ferment out in a cool place.
3) Siphon into a storage jar, top up with white wine, add 1 Campden tablet, bung tight, label and store until the wine is bright.
4) Rack into bottles, adding 1 saccharin pellet to each. Mature for 9 months and serve the wine cold at lunch, picnics or parties.

ORANGE WINE

thinly pared rind and juice of 4 Seville and 4 Navel oranges
4 very ripe bananas, peeled and mashed
250 g/8 oz sultanas, washed and chopped
3.75 litres/7½ pints cold water
5 ml/1 tsp pectic enzyme
1 Campden tablet
activated sherry flor wine yeast
2.5 ml/½ tsp nutrient
1.5 kg/3 lb white sugar

1) Place the orange parings, juice, bananas and sultanas in a bin containing the water, enzyme and 1 crushed Campden tablet. Cover and leave in a warm place for 24 hours.
2) Stir in the yeast and nutrient, and ferment on the pulp for 4 days, keeping the fruit submerged and the bin covered.
3) Strain out, press dry and discard the pulp, stir in half the sugar, and pour the must into a fermentation jar. Plug the neck with cotton wool instead of an airlock and ferment for 7 days.
4) Remove some of the must, stir in half the remaining sugar, return the must to the jar, replace the cotton wool and leave for another 10 days.
5) Repeat this process with the last portion of sugar and ferment out.
6) Siphon the young wine from its sediment into a storage jar, leaving an air gap in the jar. Plug the neck with cotton wool again, label and store in a cool place until the wine is bright.
7) Rack again, thereby increasing the air gap slightly. Replace the cotton wool and mature for 18 months in bulk before bottling. Serve this dry sherry-style wine cool, as an apéritif, or blend it after 12 months in bulk storage.

Note No acid or tannin is required.

ORCHARD TABLE WINE

2.25 kg/4½ lb unpeeled eating apples, washed and chopped
1 kg/2 lb cooking apples, washed and chopped
1 kg/2 lb hard pears, washed and chopped
500 g/1 lb quinces, washed and chopped
500 g/1 lb crabapples (John Downie), washed and chopped
2 litres/4 pints cold water
5 ml/1 tsp pectic enzyme
5 ml/1 tsp citric acid
2 Campden tablets
250 g/8 oz concentrated white grape juice
active Champagne wine yeast
2.5 ml/½ tsp nutrient
875 g/1¾ lb white sugar

1) Drop the fruit into a bin containing the water, enzyme, acid and 1 crushed Campden tablet. Cover and leave in a warm place for 24 hours while the enzyme works.
2) Stir in the concentrated grape juice, yeast and nutrient, and ferment on the pulp for 7 days, keeping the fruit submerged and the bin covered.
3) Strain out, press dry and discard the pulp, stir in the sugar, pour the must into a fermentation jar, top up if necessary, fit an airlock and ferment out.
4) Siphon the clearing wine into a sterilized storage jar, top up, add 1 Campden tablet, bung tight, label and store in a cold place until the wine is bright.
5) Rack again and mature this wine in bulk for at least 1 year before bottling. Add 1 saccharin pellet per bottle, if necessary, to take the edge off the dryness. Serve cold as a white table wine.

Note No tannin is required for this recipe.

PEACH TABLE WINE

2.25 kg/4½ lb ripe peaches, washed, stoned, skinned and sliced
3.75 litres/7½ pints cold water
10 ml/2 tsps citric acid
5 ml/1 tsp pectic enzyme
2 Campden tablets
2.5 ml/½ tsp grape tannin
250 g/8 oz concentrated white grape juice
activated Sauternes wine yeast
2.5 ml/½ tsp nutrient
1 kg/2 lb white sugar

1) Put the peaches in a bin containing the water, acid, pectic enzyme and 1 crushed Campden tablet. Cover and leave in a warm place for 24 hours while the enzyme works.
2) Add the tannin, grape juice, yeast and nutrient, and ferment on the pulp for 5 days, keeping the fruit submerged and the bin covered.
3) Strain out and discard the pulp, stir in the sugar, pour the must into a fermentation jar, top up if necessary, fit an airlock and ferment out.
4) Siphon the clearing wine into a storage jar, top up, add 1 Campden tablet, bung tight, label and store until the wine is bright.
5) Rack again and mature for 1 year, then bottle and sweeten to taste with saccharin. Serve it cold with the pudding or dessert course of a meal, or as a social wine.

PLUM AND APPLE TABLE WINE

1.5 kg/3 lb ripe black plums or damsons, washed, stoned and crushed
3 kg/6 lb mixed, unpeeled cooking and eating apples, washed and chopped
2 litres/4 pints cold water
5 ml/1 tsp citric acid
5 ml/1 tsp pectic enzyme
2 Campden tablets
250 g/8 oz concentrated red grape juice
2.5 ml/½ tsp grape tannin
activated Burgundy wine yeast
2.5 ml/½ tsp nutrient
875 g/1¾ lb white sugar

1) Put the fruit in a bin containing the water, acid, pectic enzyme and crushed Campden tablet. Cover and leave in a warm place for 24 hours while the enzyme works.
2) Stir in the grape juice, tannin, yeast and nutrient, and ferment on the pulp for 6 days, keeping the fruit submerged and the bin covered.
3) Strain out, press dry and discard the fruit, stir in the sugar, pour the must into a fermentation jar, top up if necessary, fit an airlock and ferment out.
4) Siphon the clearing wine into a storage jar, top up, add 1 Campden tablet, bung tight, label and store until the wine is bright.
5) Rack again and mature in bulk for 1 year before bottling. Serve as a dry red table wine.

PRUNE WINE

2.25 kg/4½ lb large prunes, washed and stoned
500 g/1 lb raisins, washed and chopped
pared rind and juice of 2 large lemons
4.4 litres/9 pints hot water
10 ml/2 tsps citric acid
5 ml/1 tsp pectic enzyme
1 Campden tablet
5 ml/1 tsp grape tannin
activated sherry flor wine yeast
2.5 ml/½ tsp nutrient
1 kg/2 lb white sugar

1) Place the prunes, raisins, lemon parings and juice in a bin, pour over hot water, cover and cool.
2) Add the acid, enzyme and the crushed Campden tablet. Cover and leave for 24 hours.
3) Stir in the tannin, yeast and nutrient, and ferment on the pulp for 6 days, keeping the fruit submerged and the bin covered.
4) Strain out, press dry and discard the pulp, stir in one-third of the sugar, and pour the must into a fermentation jar. Plug the neck with cotton wool instead of an airlock and ferment for 10 days.
5) Remove some of the must, stir in another third of the sugar, return the must to the jar, replace the cotton wool and leave for another 10 days.
6) Repeat this process with the last portion of sugar and ferment out.
7) Siphon the young wine from its sediment into a storage jar, leaving an air gap in the jar. Plug the neck with cotton wool again, label and store in a cool place until the wine is bright.
8) Rack again, thereby increasing the air gap slightly. Replace the cotton wool and mature for 18 months in bulk before bottling. Serve this sherry-style wine, cool as an apéritif, or blend after 12 months' bulk storage.

RHUBARB TABLE WINE

2.25 kg/4½ lb rhubarb, topped, tailed, washed and chopped small
3.75 litres/7½ pints cold water
thinly pared rind and juice of 1 lemon
2 Campden tablets
5 ml/1 tsp pectic enzyme
250 g/8 oz concentrated white grape juice
2.5 ml/½ tsp grape tannin
activated Champagne wine yeast
2.5 ml/½ tsp nutrient
1 kg/2 lb white sugar

1) Put the rhubarb in a bin containing the water, the rind and strained juice of the lemon, 1 crushed Campden tablet and pectic enzyme. Cover and leave in a warm place for 24 hours while the enzyme works.
2) Add the grape juice, tannin, yeast and nutrient, then ferment on the pulp for 5 days, keeping the fruit submerged and the bin covered.
3) Strain out, press dry and discard the pulp. Stir in the sugar, pour the must into a fermentation jar, top up if necessary, fit an airlock and ferment out.
4) Siphon the clearing wine into a storage jar, top up, add 1 Campden tablet, bung tight, label and store in a cold place until the wine is bright.
5) Rack again and mature for 1 year, then bottle and serve as a dry white table wine.

Note Gather the rhubarb in late May or early June.

RHUBARB SPARKLING WINE

2.25 kg/4½ lb rhubarb, topped, tailed, washed and
  chopped small
3.75 litres/7½ pints cold water
thinly pared rind and juice of 1 lemon
2 Campden tablets
5 ml/1 tsp pectic enzyme
250 g/8 oz concentrated white grape juice
2.5 ml/½ tsp grape tannin
activated Champagne wine yeast
2.5 ml/½ tsp nutrient
1 kg/2 lb white sugar
75 g/2½ oz caster sugar
additional activated Champagne wine yeast

1) Put the rhubarb in a bin containing the water, the rind
   and strained juice of the lemon, 1 crushed Campden
   tablet and the pectic enzyme. Cover and leave in a
   warm place for 24 hours while the enzyme works.
2) Add the grape juice, tannin, yeast and nutrient, then
   ferment on the pulp for 5 days, keeping the fruit
   submerged and the bin covered.
3) Strain out, press dry and discard the pulp. Stir in the
   white sugar, pour the must into a fermentation jar, top
   up if necessary, fit an airlock and ferment out.
4) Siphon the clearing wine into a storage jar, top up,
   add 1 Campden tablet, bung tight, label and store in a
   cold place for 6 months until the wine is bright.
5) Mix the caster sugar, additional Champagne wine
   yeast and a pinch of nutrient into the jar, fit an airlock
   and leave in a warm place for a few hours.
6) As soon as fermentation starts, siphon the wine into
   sterilized champagne bottles.
7) Fit hollow-domed or blister stoppers, wire them on and
   leave the bottles on their sides for at least 6 months
   before disgorging the secondary sediment.
8) When disgorging, add 1 or 2 saccharin pellets before
   fitting a clean stopper.

RICE AND RAISIN WINE

4 litres/8 pints hot water
500 g/1 lb coarsely crushed rice
500 g/1 lb raisins, washed and chopped
10 ml/2 tsps citric acid
activated Sauternes wine yeast
2.5 ml/½ tsp nutrient
1 kg/2 lb white sugar
1 Campden tablet

1) Pour boiling water on to the rice and raisins in a bin,
   stir well, cover and leave to cool.
2) Stir in the citric acid, yeast and nutrient, and ferment
   on the pulp for 6 days, keeping the fruit submerged and
   the bin covered.
3) Strain out the solids, stir in the sugar, pour the must
   into a fermentation jar, top up if necessary, fit an
   airlock and ferment out.
4) Siphon the clearing wine into a storage jar, top up,
   add 1 Campden tablet, bung tight, label and store
   until the wine is bright.
5) Rack again, mature in bulk for 6 months, then bottle.
   Serve as a social wine with sweet biscuits.

Note Pectic enzyme and tannin are not required.

ROSE-HIP WINE

1.75 kg/3½ lb freshly gathered rose-hips, stalked, washed and crushed
3.75 litres/7½ pints hot water
250 g/8 oz concentrated white grape juice
10 ml/2 tsps citric acid
2.5 ml/½ tsp grape tannin
activated Sauternes wine yeast
2.5 ml/½ tsp nutrient
1 kg/2 lb white sugar
1 Campden tablet

1) Place the hips in a bin, pour on the hot water, cover and leave to cool.
2) Stir in the grape juice, acid, tannin, yeast and nutrient, and ferment on the pulp for 6 days, keeping the hips submerged.
3) Strain out and press the hips dry, stir in the sugar, pour the must into a fermentation jar, top up if necessary, fit an airlock and ferment out.
4) Siphon the clearing wine into a storage jar, top up, add 1 Campden tablet, bung tight, label and store in a cool place until the wine is bright.
5) Rack again and mature in bulk for 1 year before bottling. Sweeten to taste with saccharin pellets. Serve cold as a social wine with sweet cake.

Note Gather the rose-hips in late October. Pectic enzyme is not required.

SLOE TABLE WINE

2.25 kg/4½ lb fresh ripe sloes, stalked, washed and squashed
250 g/8 oz raisins, washed and chopped
4.4 litres/9 pints hot water
10 ml/2 tsps citric acid
5 ml/1 tsp pectic enzyme
2 Campden tablets
activated Burgundy wine yeast
2.5 ml/½ tsp nutrient
1 kg/2 lb white sugar

1) Place the squashed sloes (be careful not to break the stones) and raisins in a bin, pour on the hot water, cover and leave to cool.
2) Stir in the acid, enzyme and 1 crushed Campden tablet, cover and leave for 24 hours while the enzyme works.
3) Stir in the yeast and nutrient, and ferment on the pulp for 5 days, keeping the fruit submerged and the bin covered.
4) Strain out, press dry and discard the fruit, stir in the sugar, pour the must into a fermentation jar, top up if necessary, fit an airlock and ferment out.
5) Siphon the clearing wine into a storage jar, top up, add 1 Campden tablet, bung tight, label and store in a cool place until the wine is bright.
6) Rack again, then mature this wine in bulk for 1 year before bottling for 6 months. Serve it free from chill as a dry red table wine.

Note Tannin is not required for this recipe.

SUMMER FRUIT WINE

2.25 kg/4½ lb mixed soft fruit: blackberries, black/red/
    white currants, apricots, bananas, greengages, cherries,
    gooseberries, raspberries, strawberries, peaches and
    sultana grapes, stalked, washed, stoned and mashed
3.75 litres/7½ pints hot water
5 ml/1 tsp pectic enzyme
2 Campden tablets
250 g/8 oz concentrated white grape juice
activated Sauternes wine yeast
2.5 ml/½ tsp nutrient
1 kg/2 lb sugar

1)   Place the fruit in a bin, pour on the hot water, cover
     and leave to cool.
2)   Add the pectic enzyme and 1 crushed Campden tablet,
     replace the cover and leave for 24 hours.
3)   Add the grape juice, yeast and nutrient, then ferment
     on the pulp for 5 days, keeping the fruit submerged and
     the bin covered.
4)   Strain out, press dry and discard the pulp, stir in the
     sugar, pour the must into a fermentation jar, top up if
     necessary, fit an airlock and ferment out.
5)   Siphon the clearing wine into a storage jar, top up,
     add 1 Campden tablet, bung tight, label and store in a
     cool place until the wine is bright.
6)   Rack again and mature in bulk for 1 year, then bottle
     and serve as a dry table wine, or sweeten to taste with
     saccharin and serve as a social wine.

Note Use as many different fruits as possible, ensuring only
that no one fruit predominates. No acid or tannin is
required for this recipe.

CANNED FRUIT WINES

Cans of fruit in sugar syrup make enjoyable, light, fast maturing wines. The precise quantity of fruit and syrup is not critical.

1.5 kg/3 lb canned apricots, golden plums and gooseberries
  in equal measure
3.3 litres/6½ pints cold water
10 ml/2 tsps citric acid
5 ml/1 tsp pectic enzyme
2 Campden tablets
250 g/8 oz concentrated white grape juice
2.5 ml/½ tsp grape tannin
activated German wine yeast
2.5 ml/½ tsp nutrient
875 g/1¾ lb white sugar

1) Strain off the syrup from the fruit into a sterilized bottle and store in a refrigerator for later use.
2) Mash the fruit in a bin, discard the stones, pour on the cold water and stir in the acid, pectic enzyme and 1 crushed Campden tablet. Cover and leave in a warm place for 24 hours while the enzyme works.
3) Stir in the grape juice, reserved syrup, tannin, the yeast and nutrient. Ferment on the pulp for 3 days, keeping the fruit submerged and the bin covered.
4) Strain out the pulp, roll it around in a nylon straining bag but do not press before discarding it. Stir in the sugar, pour the must into a fermentation jar, top up, fit an airlock and ferment out.
5) Siphon the clearing wine into a storage jar, top up, add 1 Campden tablet, bung tight, label and store until the wine is bright.
6) Rack into bottles, label and store until the wine is 3 months old. Serve cold as a luncheon or social wine.

Note Canned fruits do not make good dessert wines.

VARIATION

Use approximately 1.5 kg/3 lb of any single canned fruit in sugar syrup or combination of fruits to make different but attractive light table wines.

DRIED FRUIT WINES

Currants, sultanas, raisins, muscatels, apricots, dates, figs and prunes are the most suitable. The dried fruit is about one-quarter of the weight of the fresh fruit, eg 250 g/8 oz raisins are the equivalent of 1 kg/2 lb of fresh grapes. The flavour of apricots and figs is very strong so they must be used sparingly. 375 g/12 oz apricots or 250 g/8 oz figs are normally enough for 5 litres/1 gallon must. Approximately two-thirds the weight of dried grapes consists of fermentable sugar.

2.25 kg/4½ lb currants, sultanas, raisins, muscatels or
  mixed dried fruit, washed and chopped
3.75 litres/7½ pints hot water
5 ml/1 tsp citric acid
5 ml/1 tsp pectic enzyme
2 Campden tablets
activated wine yeast
2.5 ml/½ tsp nutrient

1) Place the fruit in a bin, pour on the hot water, cover and leave to cool.
2) Stir in the acid, enzyme and 1 crushed Campden tablet, cover and leave in a warm place for 24 hours.
3) Stir in the yeast and nutrient, and ferment out on the pulp, keeping the fruit submerged and the bin covered.
4) Strain out, press dry and discard the fruit, pour the young wine into a storage jar, top up if necessary, add 1 Campden tablet, bung tight, label and store in a cold place until the wine is clear.
5) Rack again and store in bulk for 1 year before bottling. Serve this wine cold as a mid morning or afternoon wine.

Note No sugar is normally required in this recipe.
Do not include dried peel amongst the dried fruit.

VARIATION

With 250 g/8 oz figs, use also 500 g/1 lb sultanas and 1 kg/2 lb white sugar.

FRUIT JUICE WINES

Unsweetened pure fruit juices are widely available in supermarkets and can be made into attractive wines.

2 litres/4 pints apple juice
1 litre/2 pints grapefruit juice
250 g/8 oz concentrated white grape juice
1 litre/2 pints cold water
5 ml/1 tsp pectic enzyme
activated Champagne or Hock wine yeast
2.5 ml/½ tsp nutrient
1 kg/2 lb white sugar
1 Campden tablet

1) Empty the fruit juices into a sterilized fermentation jar, add the concentrated grape juice dissolved in the water, stir in the pectic enzyme, yeast and nutrient, leave room for the sugar, fit an airlock and ferment for 3 days in an atmospheric temperature around 21°C/70°F.
2) Remove some of the must, stir in the sugar, return it to the jar, top up, re-fit the airlock and ferment out in a cooler place at around 16°C/61°F.
3) Siphon the wine into a storage jar, top up, add 1 Campden tablet, bung tight, label and leave until the wine is bright.
4) Rack into bottles, label and store for a further 3 or 4 months. Sweeten to taste with saccharin if required.

VARIATIONS

Apricot nectar, orange juice, passion-fruit juice or pineapple juice may be used instead of the grapefruit juice. It is, however, best to keep to the apple juice base, otherwise the flavours become too strong. No additional acid is required. Tomato juice is *not* suitable.

JAM WINES

Pure jams and jellies that are free from additional pectin, colouring and preservative may be used to make very pleasant light table and social wines.

1.5 kg/3 lb redcurrant jelly
3.75 litres/7½ pints warm water
10 ml/2 tsps pectic enzyme
10 ml/2 tsps citric acid
2 Campden tablets
250 g/8 oz concentrated rosé grape juice
2.5 ml/½ tsp grape tannin
activated Bordeaux wine yeast
2.5 ml/½ tsp nutrient
500 g/1 lb white sugar

1) Dissolve the jelly in the warm water in a bin and leave to cool.
2) Add the pectic enzyme, acid and 1 crushed Campden tablet, cover and leave in a warm place for 24 hours while the enzyme works.
3) Stir in the grape juice, tannin, yeast and nutrient. Pour the must into a fermentation jar, leaving room for the sugar, fit an airlock and ferment for 8 days.
4) Remove some of the must, stir in the sugar, return it to the jar, top up, re-fit the airlock and ferment out.
5) Siphon the clearing wine into a storage jar, top up, add 1 Campden tablet, bung tight, label and store until the wine is bright.
6) Rack into bottles, label and store for 6 months.

VARIATIONS

Bramble jelly, apricot, raspberry and strawberry jams are all equally successful.

SERVING WINE

Good wine needs good company to be enjoyed to the full; there is diminished pleasure in drinking wine alone.

The most important factor in serving your wine well is the choice of the wine itself. It must be a good example of its type – mature, clear, of fine colour, and completely free from off flavours. It must be suitable for the occasion, harmonizing both with the food and with the company.

Temperature

Red table wines and dessert wines should be served at room temperature, ie free from chill. This is generally reckoned to be about 18°C/65°F. Bring the wine from your store into the kitchen the previous day and stand the bottle upright so that any sediment in the bottle has time to settle.

Apéritifs, white and rosé wines need to be chilled to around 10°C/50°F before serving them. Stand the bottle in the door compartment of the refrigerator for an hour or so, or place it in a bucket of water containing crushed ice for 10–20 minutes. If the wine is too cold, the esters and volatile acids which form the bouquet and the greeting will be inhibited, and the wine will lose much of its attraction. If it is not cold enough, the wine will taste soft and flabby.

Sparkling wines should be cooled a little more, to about 7°C/45°F. By chilling sparkling wines, you hold back the release of the carbon dioxide gas, and the bubbles continue to rise in the glass for a much longer period.

Decanting

Before you serve your wine, it should be decanted from the bottle in which it has matured into a clear glass decanter. This is beneficial to all but sparkling wines for a number of reasons.

a) The aesthetic appeal of wine in a decanter is greater than in a bottle.

b) Decanting a wine allows it to "breathe" for a little while before you drink it. After a wine has been bottled for a year or so, many chemical changes have taken place. Some of these will have produced attractive smelling esters and volatile acids which are temporarily combined in the wine. When the cork is drawn and the wine carefully poured into a decanter or glass carafe, these aromatic elements are slowly released. After some time, varying from one to several hours, depending on the wine, the bouquet will have developed and the wine will be much enhanced. Young wines take longest to develop.

c) Quite often a wine throws a further deposit while in a bottle. By decanting it carefully, the clear wine can be separated from the lees. Withdraw the cork carefully, wipe the lip of the bottle with a clean cloth, hold the bottle firmly by the waist in one hand and hold the decanter or carafe in the other. Raise the bottle towards a source of light, move the lip towards the decanter or carafe until they touch, and pour the wine carefully down the inside wall. Continue pouring until the sediment has slid slowly up the side of the bottle and is just about to reach the neck. Return the bottle to an upright position, but do not throw away the dregs; they make a most useful and interesting addition to meat gravy.

Glasses

Different sizes of glasses are usually used for different wines, but they should all have a number of common features. For still wines, each should be of clear glass, free of colour, heavy cutting or engraving. They should have a stem and base, and be incurved at the top to retain the bouquet. The

Correct glasses enhance wines and enable the wine drinker to focus totally on their aroma and colour without any unnecessary distraction.

purpose of a wine glass is to hold the wine rather like a frame holds a picture. It should concentrate one's attention on the wine without distraction by its own fussiness.

If the glass has straight sides, or if, even worse, they lean outwards, the bouquet will be dissipated much more rapidly. Similarly, unless the bowl is made from clear, undecorated glass, the colour and clarity of the wine will be impaired. To obtain the best from your wine, you have to be able to enjoy it with your sense of smell as well as your sense of sight. An incurving plain glass bowl helps these two senses to enjoy these features to the full.

The stem of the glass supports the bowl, holding it up to sight rather as the stem of a flower holds up the floret. It provides you with a "handle," so that you can pick up the glass without touching the bowl and covering it with finger marks. The stem should be long and strong enough to serve this purpose.

The base should be broad enough to balance the bowl and stem safely, and to enable you to hold the glass comfortably. Having picked up a glass by its stem, it should be held firmly by its base, the thumb on top and the fingers

underneath. This will enable you to hold the glass up to the light to please your visual sense, and to swirl the wine slowly to release its bouquet and so please your sense of smell.

Sparkling wines, on the other hand, should be served in a tall flute-shaped glass so that the most can be made of the sparkling bubbles; a wide saucer-shaped glass is not suitable. Fill the glass three-quarters full.

On the dinner table, glasses show up best on a white damask cloth. When handed round, as at a cocktail party, they should be served from a silver salver, a mirrored glass tray or on a tray covered by a damask napkin. Do not use a painted tray, no matter how beautiful, nor anything that is colourful in any way. It detracts from the beauty of the wine and diminishes its effect.

Before use, glasses should be polished with a clean, dry linen cloth to ensure that they sparkle and are totally free from finger marks, washing-up marks, and so on. When stored, they should be stood upright, so that they do not absorb into the bowl the smell of polish, varnish or wood from the shelf on which they stand.

53

Pouring the Wine

When pouring wine into a glass, do it slowly and with care, to ensure that none is spilled and that the glasses do not contain too much. The glass should be between half and two-thirds full. A glass less than half full looks mean, but a glass full to the brim cannot be moved without spilling it, and the wine in it cannot be savoured because there is no room for your nose! Furthermore, a glass of wine between half and two-thirds full has the most aesthetic appeal.

Drinking Wine

Since the most important time for drinking is with meals, you should exercise your greatest skill in matching your wines with the food. If you plan your winemaking thoughtfully you will make a variety of wines suitable for use as apéritifs, for table purposes – red, white and rosé, some sweeter white wines to accompany the dessert course, some sweet and fortified wines to follow the meal, a sparkling wine for that special occasion which may occur unexpectedly, and some wines that are best defined as 'social wines'.

Social wines are for drinking while enjoying conversation with family or friends, perhaps nibbling a savoury biscuit, or simply watching television. They should not normally be too dry, sweet, strong, thin or too much of anything. They do not even have to be too good, since they would then deserve more attention than the occasion affords. They may be red, white or rosé, still or lively. A lively wine has a few bubbles of carbon dioxide rising slowly, although it is far from being a fully sparkling wine; it can be delightful when served cool on a warm evening.

A glass of wine can be most enjoyable at mid morning. It is different from the apéritif one drinks before a meal. Such a wine can be very dry and gentle, or even just a little sweet; the flavour needs to be gentle too. A rosé, for example, served cold and fresh, makes an unusual and surprisingly enjoyable refresher. A glass of a Madeira-type wine with a piece of cake in mid afternoon is equally pleasant.

Another time when wine can be especially enjoyable is last thing at night. A couple of glasses of wine and a few biscuits make an ideal nightcap. There is no more pleasant soporific than wine!

BREWING BEER AT HOME

Ales and beers have been brewed in the home for centuries. They were originally brewed by women as part of their everyday work of providing food and drink for their menfolk and children. The same leaven of yeast was used both for baking and brewing. At first, ale was simply brewed from a weak malt solution made from wheat or barley. Occasionally, nettles, yarrow or some other herb might be added to give it a different flavour; alternatively, honey might be added both for flavour and strength. Later, when hops were added, the brew was called beer. Today, the words ale and beer are interchangeable and hops are the only flavouring and preservative used.

Towards the end of the nineteenth-century, Gladstone levied a licence and a tax on home-brewed beer, thereby virtually ending this aspect of the craft. The law was not repealed until 1963 but it signalled a great upsurge in home-brewing. By 1970, major companies had marketed cans of malt extract (malt syrup) flavoured with hop essence that could be converted into beer with very little trouble. One firm even included a large polythene bag in which to brew the beer.

In recent years, the quality of the malt extract and flavouring has improved considerably and superb kits are widely available. Many home-brew centres also stock a variety of malted barleys, adjuncts and several varieties of hops for the enthusiasts who want to brew their beer in the traditional manner.

Hygiene

This is just as important in home-brewing as it is in winemaking. Every piece of equipment should be washed clean and sterilized before use, as described on page 8. Ingredients do not need sterilizing but it is important to use only those of good quality to obtain the best results.

Stages in Beer Making/Brewing

As in winemaking, there are three stages in home brewing – Preparation, Fermentation and Maturation.

Preparation includes the sterilization of the equipment, dissolving malt extract in warm water, boiling hops and cooling the strained wort. It includes the addition of adjuncts when used, and the mashing of the grains if the malt solution is also being prepared at home.

Fermentation begins with the activation and pitching of the yeast into the cooled wort, maintenance of the proper temperature, the skimming of the dirty froth, removal of the yeast line around the bin and the stirring of the brew. It also includes any dry hopping and continues until fermentation ceases.

Maturation begins with the addition of finings if used, the clarification of the beer in a cold atmosphere, racking into sterilized bottles or casks, priming with sugar, the addition of lactose if used, and the sealing of the bottles and casks. It includes also storage of the beer, first in a warm room and then in a cool place, for at least three or four weeks to obtain the best results.

Beer styles

The most popular beer style is bitter. It is usually divided into three sub styles – light ale, pale ale, and export ale.

Light ale has a low original specific gravity of around 1.030. It should be a golden straw colour.

Pale ale has an original specific gravity of about 1.036. The colour should be a light amber.

Export ale is also known as India pale ale, best bitter or Burton-type. It should have an original specific gravity of between 1.040 and 1.044, be a bright copper colour and have a malty taste and a tangy hop bitterness.

Dry stout is sometimes called Irish stout and should be jet

black in colour, bone dry, full bodied and bitter flavoured. The original specific gravity should be around 1.044.

Sweet stout is less strong than dry stout, its original specific gravity being 1.036. Fewer hops are required to balance the lower alcohol and the beer should be sweetened with lactose.

Brown ale varies in different parts of Great Britain. The colour ranges from dark amber to brown black. The original specific gravity is low at 1.030, fewer hops are used and a little lactose can be added to sweeten the ale.

Barley wine is as strong as a table wine and should be fermented from an original specific gravity of around 1.090. The colour may vary from a dark gold to a dark copper brown. The flavour is more malty than hoppy, the texture very smooth from long maturation. Hard water and a Champagne wine yeast help in flavour development.

Lager is very difficult to make at home and most attempts are more like a pale ale than a Pilsen lager. It is essential to use soft water, a Continental malt, Continental hops such as Hallertau, Saaz or Styrian, a Carlsbergensis yeast, a low fermentation temperature, and to store the beer for at least three months. The original specific gravity should be around 1.044.

Equipment

Purpose-made utensils are readily obtainable for mashing, fermenting and storing both draught and bottled beers.

Polythene bins. The same as those used in winemaking, are ideal for brewing beer. Always use a bin larger than the quantity of beer being brewed to allow for the development of a frothy head during fermentation.

Long plastic stirring spoon. This is needed for stirring the brew, together with polythene funnels.

Sparging bag. Made of calico, this is used for straining hops and grains. Any straining device made of a fine mesh can be substituted if a sparging bag is not available.

Siphon. This is needed for transferring the brew into bottles or a cask.

Beer bottles. Only proper returnable-type beer bottles should be used. It is unwise to use mineral water or cider bottles since these are not made strong enough to withstand the pressure created by the priming fermentation.

Stoppers. Screw-in stoppers should have new rubber washers. New crown caps should be used to seal other bottles. Crown caps require a crimping tool to fit them tightly on to the bottles.

Stainless steel or aluminium boiling pan. This will be needed for boiling the hops and wort; it should be large. Iron and chipped enamel vessels should be avoided. A pressure cooker is useful for boiling the hops.

Plastic casks. These are available in various sizes for draught beer. Some are fitted with ingenious devices to keep the beer in good condition. Others are fitted with carbon dioxide injectors in the same way as soda water bottles.

Immersion heaters. This is particularly useful for home brewers who wish to mash their own grains or brew large quantities. The heater should be controlled by an adjustable thermostat.

Insulating material. An old blanket is useful if an immersion heater is not available for mashing grains.

Other equipment. A thermometer, hydrometer and trial jar as used in winemaking will prove useful and are worth acquiring at the outset.

Ingredients

The principal ingredients for making beer are malt, hops, water and yeast.

Malt. When barley is malted, most of the grains are only lightly roasted and this malt is the basic ingredient of every beer. Some grains, however, are roasted until they are a little darker and this crystal malt is added to sharpen the flavour of a beer. Other grains are roasted until they are quite brown and some until they are black. These malts are

Opposite A selection of hops, grains and other ingredients used in beermaking.

used mainly for colouring and flavouring brown ales and stouts. Like hops, malted grains need to be kept sealed, otherwise they pick up moisture from the air and become slack. It is best to buy them as and when required and to make sure that they are crushed. It is difficult to crush the grains at home.

Malt is also available as malt extract (malt syrup) and is sometimes marketed as particularly suitable for bitter beer because it is made from the appropriate blend of barleys that have been roasted to the correct degree of colour. If you cannot obtain this, a perfectly plain malt extract will do, but make sure it contains no fish oil!

Hops. Ask for Wye Challenger (formerly Goldings) when brewing light ales and bitter beers and for Wye Northdown (formerly Fuggles) when brewing stouts and brown ales. Wye Target hops (formerly Northern Brewer) are a supplementary hop for very bitter beer. Hops are also available in pellet form, free from extraneous petals and stalks. Although perhaps more expensive, very few are needed to obtain the required degree of bitterness and are much easier to handle. They are packed in sealed sachets and keep better than loose hops which go stale when left exposed to the air.

Water. The quality of the brew depends much on the water used for mashing the grains. A soft water produces excellent stouts and brown ales, but less good light ales and bitter beers. Conversely, hard water produces excellent light ales and bitter beers but less good stouts and brown ales.

A little table salt can be added to hard water when brewing stouts, brown ales and lagers, while sachets of hardening salts can be bought to add to soft water when brewing bitters and barley wines. These are available from your local home-brew centre and contain mostly calcium and magnesium sulphates. The packet will indicate the quantity to add.

When brewing beer from malt extract, either hard or soft water can be used.

Yeast. Brewer's yeast should always be used. Different strains are available for beers, stouts and lagers. A Champagne wine yeast should be used when making barley wine. As with wine, it is best to activate the yeast before adding it to the wort.

Adjuncts. These include all items other than malt, hops, water, yeast, acid and nutrient. Apart from sugar, adjuncts can include flaked rice, oatmeal, wheat flakes, torrified barley (popcorn-like barley grains), raw grain (untreated barley), brewing flour and syrups such as maize syrup and golden syrup. They should not exceed 20% of the malt.

Sugar. This is used to increase the alcohol content. Ordinary granulated sugar is adequate, although glucose, brown sugar or golden syrup are also suitable.

Finings. These are frequently used to clear beers quickly although they will clear on their own. Of the proprietary finings, gelatine is most popular and is often added before fermentation so that it clears the beer as soon as fermentation finishes. Irish moss is sometimes added with hops at the boiling stage to ensure a clear wort to ferment. Bentonite gel and isinglass can also be used when fermentation has finished.

Citric acid and yeast nutrient. As in winemaking, the addition of citric acid and nutrient ensure the complete conversion of all the fermentable sugars. Quantities to add per 25 litres/5 gallons beer are 5 ml/1 teaspoon of citric acid and another of nutrient. Home-brewed beers will, however, be perfectly satisfactory without either.

GUIDE TO BEER MAKING

Beer from Kits

The easiest way to brew beer is from a prepared kit. There are two types – wet and dry. The most common kit available from all home-brew centres is a wet kit consisting of a container of hop-flavoured, thick malt extract adjusted to a particular style of beer – bitter, brown ale, stout, lager, barley wine etc. All that needs to be provided is some extra sugar and the water. Dry kits consist of a muslin bag of hops and grains, a polythene bag of malt flour and sachets of yeast and finings. Detailed instructions accompany each kit and vary minimally from brand to brand.

All that needs to be done to brew beer from a wet kit is to dissolve the hopped malt extract and sugar in warm water, to leave the wort to ferment with the yeast provided for about six days before siphoning it into beer bottles and then to add priming sugar before sealing. The beer is ready to drink after another week or two.

With dry kits, the hops and grains must be boiled loosely for about an hour before being strained into a solution made up of the malt flour, sugar and water. The wort is then fermented with yeast and finished off in the same way as a wet kit.

The kits are marketed in varying sizes; those new to home brewing are recommended to begin by making up a few smaller kits. The only equipment required is a natural polythene bin and cover, a plastic stirring spoon, small funnel, siphon and a number of proper beer bottles and stoppers. Larger kits are ideal for both bottling and making draught beers for which a pressure keg is required. These kegs or casks are not expensive if used regularly and are certainly worth investing in if you or your family are likely to consume more than 10 litres/20 pints of beer a week.

Making Malt Extract and Hop Beers

As soon as you have acquired the knack of brewing and feel confident enough to experiment, brew this basic recipe for 10 litres/20 pints of a bitter beer and then make up your own variations to taste.

BASIC MALT EXTRACT BITTER BEER

40 g/1½ oz Wye Challenger (Goldings) hops
9.4 litres/19 pints water
1 kg/2 lb malt extract
500 g/1 lb light brown sugar
activated beer yeast

1) Boil the hops in some of the water in a large pan for between 45–60 minutes, keeping the pan covered to retain as much flavour as possible. Use a rolling boil.
   Alternatively
   Cook the hops for 15 minutes in a pressure cooker at maximum pressure.

2) When the boiling is finished, leave the hops to settle for about 30 minutes.

3) Meanwhile, heat 1.2 litres/2½ pints of the water and dissolve the malt extract and sugar in it.

4) Strain the liquor from the hops through a fine nylon sieve on to the wort in a polythene bin.

5) Rinse the hops with some warm water and strain again through the sieve on to the wort.

6) Discard the hops and top up the bin with cold water to a total of 10 litres/20 pints to allow for wastage when racking. Leave the wort to cool.

7) If you have a hydrometer, check the specific gravity of the wort; it should be around 1.040.

8) When the temperature has fallen to below 21°C/70°F, stir well and pitch the activated yeast. Cover the bin and leave it overnight in a suitable position where the temperature is about 18°C/65°F.

   Note To activate the yeast, remove 300 ml/10 oz of the wort from the bin and add an equal quantity of cold water. Stir in the yeast, cover and leave in a warm position (24°C/75°F) for about an hour. Stir occasionally to encourage the absorption of oxygen from the air. If the yeast is viable, fermentation will soon start and a froth will be formed. The yeast starter can be pitched into the wort as soon as required.

Recipe continues over.

9) Next day, skim off the dirty froth and rouse the wort thoroughly to get rid of any dissolved carbon dioxide and to admit some air to encourage the yeast to grow. Replace the cover and leave the brew for another 24 hours.

10) Repeat the skimming and stirring next day, remembering to wipe the yeast ring from the side of the bin at the surface of the wort. Replace the cover and leave the brew to ferment out.

11) When the surface is clear and the beer is still, in about 6 days from the start, check the gravity again; it should range between 1.002 and 1.006. Move the bin to as cool a place as possible and leave for 2 days while the sediment settles. Finings may be added at this stage if liked. Check the gravity again. If the reading remains the same, it is safe to assume that fermentation has finished, and that the beer is ready for bottling.

12) Rack the beer into sterilized beer bottles.

13) Prime the beer by adding 5 ml/1 tsp sugar per 1 litre/ 2 pints beer, then seal the bottles with screw stoppers or crown caps and shake them gently to dissolve the sugar; this also tests the seal.

14) Label the bottles and leave upright in a warm place for a few days while the sugar is fermenting, then store them in a cool place for 3 weeks while the beer matures.

Note This beer will keep for many months and improves steadily.

VARIATIONS

a) Slightly increase the malt extract and reduce the sugar. Two measures of malt extract to one of sugar is about as low a ratio as is safe to use for a good flavour. Try three to one for an even more malty flavour. Do not decrease the malt or increase the sugar as this reduces the malty flavour and increases the raw alcohol to an unacceptable degree.

b) Increase the quantity of hops slightly or add a small quantity, eg 7 g/¼ oz of another variety such as Wye Target (Northern Brewer) to make a more bitter or tangy beer.

c) Save a handful of the dry hops or a few pellets to add to the fermenting wort after the final skimming. This enhances the hoppy flavour of the brew.

d) Add some flaked maize or flaked rice, up to a maximum of 175 g/6 oz per 10 litres/20 pints beer. This increases the body as well as the tang of the beer. Some flaked barley or flaked wheat may also be used, especially for the brewing of a stronger beer. Add these various adjuncts to the hops at the outset of the boiling. First try one variety of flakes, then another, then combinations and then different quantities. Every variation will subtly alter the finished brew.

e) Substitute golden syrup for sugar. It is easier to dissolve and ferments rapidly. You will need 600 g/1¼ lb of syrup to replace 500 g/1 lb of sugar. Glucose, too, may be used in powder form, either as a total or part substitute for sugar.

Opposite Purpose-made brewing equipment is readily available and can be used repeatedly.

RECIPES BASED ON
MALT EXTRACT AND HOP BEERS

Most home-brew centres stock malt extracts suitably prepared for stouts or brown ales to which only hops, sugar, water and yeast have to be added. Alternatively, use the following recipes, based on the basic recipe for bitter beer (pages 59–60), to make 10 litres/20 pints of a dry stout or brown ale.

DRY STOUT

32 g/1¼ oz Wye Northdown (Fuggles) hops
175 g/6 oz crushed black malt grains
125 g/4 oz flaked rice
9.4 litres/19 pints water
1 kg/2 lb malt extract
500 g/1 lb dark brown sugar
activated stout yeast

1) Boil all but a handful of the hops, all the malt grains and the flaked rice in 2.5 litres/5 pints of the water in a covered pan for 45 minutes. Use a rolling boil to extract all the required constituents.
2) Leave the hops for 30 minutes while the solids settle.
3) Heat some more water and dissolve the malt extract and sugar in it.
4) Strain the hops, grain and rice liquor into it. Discard the solids.
5) Top up with the remaining cold water and leave to cool.
6) Check the specific gravity if using a hydrometer; it should read around 1.040.
7) When the temperature has fallen to 18°C/65°F, pitch an activated yeast. Cover and leave to ferment.
8) Skim and stir as for bitter beer (see pages 59–60).
9) Add the remaining hops, wetting them thoroughly so that they do not float on the surface, then ferment out.
10) Rack, prime, seal, label and store as for bitter beer (see pages 59–60).

VARIATIONS

a) Flaked oatmeal is an alternative to flaked rice.
b) To make a sweet stout, increase the water to a total of 10 litres/20 pints so that the beer is not quite so strong, and, prior to bottling, stir in 275 g/9 oz lactose – an unfermentable sugar.

BROWN ALE

25 g/1 oz Wye Northdown (Fuggles) hops
125 g/4 oz crushed malt grains
50 g/2 oz crushed black malt grains
9.4 litres/19 pints water
1 kg/2 lb malt extract
375 g/12 oz dark brown sugar
activated beer yeast

1) Boil all but a handful of the hops and all the malt grains in 2.5 litres/5 pints of water in a covered pan for 45 minutes. Use a rolling boil.
2) Leave the solids to settle for 30 minutes.
3) Heat some of the water and dissolve the malt extract and sugar in it.
4) Strain the hops and grain liquor into it. Discard the solids.
5) Top up with the remaining cold water and leave to cool.
6) Check the specific gravity if using a hydrometer; it should read around 1.030.
7) Pitch an activated yeast when the temperature of the wort has fallen to 18°C/65°F. Cover and leave to ferment.
8) Skim and stir as for bitter beer (see pages 59–60).
9) Add the remaining hops, wetting them thoroughly so that they do not float on the surface, then ferment out.
10) Rack, prime, seal, label and store as for bitter beer (see pages 59–60).
Note This beer will finish dry.

VARIATION

If a slightly sweet brown ale is preferred, include 125 g/4 oz lactose before bottling.

LAGER

4.4 litres/9 pints water
500 g/1 lb pale malt extract
175 g/6 oz white sugar
20 g/¾ oz Hallertau hops
activated Carlsbergensis yeast

1) Heat the water and dissolve the malt extract and sugar in it.
2) Add 15 g/½ oz hops and boil in a covered pan for 30 minutes. Add the rest of the hops and boil for a further 10 minutes.
3) Remove from the heat and leave to cool, covered, for 30 minutes.
4) Strain the liquor through a nylon sieve or sparging bag into a polythene bin.
5) Rinse the hops with 300 ml/10 oz of warm water and strain again on to the wort.
6) Pour the wort into a fermentation jar and leave to cool, then add the yeast. Fit an airlock and ferment in a cool place (10°C/50°F) for about 10–14 days or until no more bubbles rise in the jar even when shaken. Leave until the sediment settles.
7) Rack the beer into bottles, prime with caster sugar at the rate of 5 ml/1 tsp per 1 litre/2 pints beer, seal as described on page 60, label and store for 3 months. Serve chilled.

Making Grain-mashed Beers

Although the concentration of worts has so improved that the vast majority of home brewers use malt extract, some home-brew enthusiasts mash malted grains to produce their own malt solutions.

The character of a grain-based beer is affected by the temperature at which a brewer infuses or mashes the malt grains to convert the starch to maltose. This is the sugar which is subsequently converted into glucose and then into alcohol by the enzymes in the yeast. During the mashing a substance called dextrin is produced and the higher the mashing temperature the more dextrin is produced. Dextrin gives body and substance to a beer and a hint of sweetness. The brewer uses different coloured grains and mashes them at different temperatures to produce the different beers.

Temperature is also important during the period of fermentation. A steady 18°C/65°F is best when using a top fermenting beer yeast, but 10°C/50°F is better for a bottom fermenting Continental yeast for brewing lager. If the fermentation temperature is too high, bitterness develops in the beer.

Right *Pouring warm water over grains in a sparging bag to wash off the maltose sugar.*

BASIC GRAIN-MASHED BITTER BEER

10 litres/2½ gallons hard water
1.5 kg/3 lb crushed pale malt grains
50 g/2 oz crushed crystal malt grains
50 g/2 oz flaked maize
50 g/2 oz flaked rice
beer yeast
25 g/1 oz Wye Challenger (Goldings) hops
7 g/¼ oz Wye Target (Northern Brewer) hops
125 g/4 oz glucose powder
125 g/4 oz soft brown sugar
proprietary beer finings

1) **Mashing.** Heat half the water to 75°C/167°F, sprinkle on and stir in the pale malt, crystal malt, flaked maize and flaked rice. Cover the pan with a lid and insulating material so that a temperature of 67°C/152°F can be maintained for at least 2 hours while the ingredients are being mashed. Alternatively, mash the grains in a container fitted with an immersion heater. Rouse the grains every 30 minutes to stimulate the extraction.

2) **End point.** Check that all the starch has been converted into maltose by placing 15 ml/1 tablespoon of the liquor in a white saucer, then adding 2–3 drops of household iodine. If the colour darkens, indicating the presence of starch, continue mashing at the same temperature for another 30 minutes, then check again. Continue mashing until the end point is reached, ie until there is no change in the colour.

3) **Sparging.** Strain the liquor and grains through a calico sparging bag into a boiling pan. Pour 600 ml/20 oz of warm water over the grains in the bag to wash off the final traces of maltose sugar on them. Discard the grains.

4) Remove a cupful of wort, dilute with a cupful of cold water and use this to activate the yeast.

5) **Boiling.** Add the Challenger hops to the wort, wet them thoroughly, cover the pan and boil vigorously for 45 minutes. Add the Target hops, wetting them carefully, then continue to boil for another 15 minutes.

6) **Settling.** Remove the pan from the heat and leave it for 30 minutes for the hops and protein to settle.

7) **Straining.** Strain off the hops through the sparging bag into a polythene bin, then stir in the glucose and sugar. Check the specific gravity; it should be about 1.044.

8) Top up with cold water to 10 litres/2½ gallons. Cover and leave to cool.

9) **Pitching.** Pitch the activated yeast and stir the brew thoroughly to mix in some air as well as to distribute the yeast. Cover and leave for 24 hours in a temperature of 18°C/65°F.

10) **Skimming.** Skim off the dirty froth and remove the yeast ring around the bin. Rouse the brew thoroughly to admit some air.

11) Repeat this process on the next day, then leave the beer to finish fermenting.

12) **Fining.** Stir in the finings in the quantity recommended by the manufacturer and move the bin to a cold place for 2 days while the sediment settles.

13) **Bottling.** Rack the beer into sterilized beer bottles.

14) Prime with caster sugar at the rate of 5 ml/1 tsp per 1 litre/2 pints beer, then seal and label.

15) Mature this beer for at least 1 month, and preferably 3 months, since it improves steadily.

VARIATIONS

Vary as for malt extract and hop beers (see page 60).

RECIPES BASED ON GRAIN-MASHED BEERS

The basic recipe on page 65 can be used to make the following beers.

The quantity of hops, malt and other ingredients in the recipes can all be varied according to taste, thereby producing subtle but important differences in flavour.

DRY STOUT

10 litres/2½ gallons soft water
1 kg/2 lb crushed pale malt grains
125 g/4 oz crushed crystal malt grains
75 g/3 oz crushed black malt grains
50 g/2 oz flaked oatmeal
50 g/2 oz wheat flakes
beer yeast
25 g/1 oz Wye Northdown (Fuggles) hops
125 g/4 oz glucose powder
125 g/4 oz soft brown sugar
proprietary beer finings

1) Heat half the water to 75°C/167°F, sprinkle on and stir in the grains, oatmeal and wheat flakes. Cover with a lid and insulating material so that a temperature of 64°C/147°F can be maintained for at least 2 hours while the ingredients are being mashed. Rouse the grains every 30 minutes.
2) Check until end point is reached.
3) Sparge the liquor and grains, then discard the grains.
4) Activate the yeast as directed on page 65.
5) Add the hops to the wort, wetting them thoroughly, cover, and boil vigorously for 45 minutes.
6) Remove the pan from the heat, and leave the hops and protein for 30 minutes to settle.
7) Strain the hops into a polythene bin, then stir in the glucose and sugar. Check the specific gravity; it should be about 1.044.
8) Top up with cold water to 10 litres/2½ gallons, then cover and cool.
9) Pitch the activated yeast and stir thoroughly. Cover and leave for 24 hours in a temperature of 18°C/65°F.
10) Skim off the dirty froth and remove the yeast ring. Rouse the brew thoroughly.
11) Repeat next day, and leave to finish fermenting.
12) Stir in the finings as directed by the manufacturer and leave in a cold place for 2 days.
13) Rack into sterilized beer bottles.
14) Prime with caster sugar as for bitter grain-mashed beer (see page 65), then seal and label.
15) Mature for 1–3 months.

BROWN ALE

10 litres/2½ gallons soft water
1 kg/2 lb crushed pale malt grains
125 g/4 oz crushed crystal malt grains
75 g/3 oz crushed chocolate malt grains
50 g/2 oz flaked oatmeal
50 g/2 oz wheat flakes
beer yeast
25 g/1 oz Wye Northdown (Fuggles) hops
125 g/4 oz glucose powder
125 g/4 oz soft brown sugar
proprietary beer finings

1) Heat half the water to 75°C/167°F, sprinkle on and stir in the grains, oatmeal and wheat flakes. Cover with a lid and insulating material so that a temperature of 64°C/147°F can be maintained for at least 2 hours. Rouse the grains every 30 minutes.
2) Check until end point is reached.
3) Sparge the liquor and grains, then discard the grains.
4) Activate the yeast as directed on page 65.
5) Add the hops to the wort, wetting them thoroughly, then cover and boil vigorously for 45 minutes.
6) Leave the hops and protein to settle off heat for 30 minutes.
7) Strain into a polythene bin, then stir in the glucose and sugar. Check the specific gravity; it should be about 1.044.
8) Top up with cold water to 10 litres/2½ gallons, then cover and cool.
9) Pitch the activated yeast and stir the brew thoroughly. Cover and leave for 24 hours in a temperature of 18°C/65°F.
10) Skim off the dirty froth and remove the yeast ring. Rouse the brew thoroughly.
11) Repeat on the next day, and leave to finish fermenting.
12) Stir in the finings as directed by the manufacturer and leave in a cold place for 2 days.
13) Rack into sterilized beer bottles.
14) Prime with caster sugar as for bitter grain-mashed beer (see page 65), then seal and label.
15) Mature for 1–3 months.

BARLEY WINE

5 litres/1¼ gallons hard water
2.5 kg/5 lb crushed pale malt grains
40 g/1½ oz Wye Challenger (Goldings) hops
250 g/8 oz glucose chips
activated ale and Champagne yeasts

1) Heat 3.75 litres/8 pints of the water to 65.5°C/150°F, and mash the malt grains in this for 2 hours, rousing them every 30 minutes.
2) Check for end point as described on page 65, and continue mashing if necessary until the end point is reached.
3) Strain out and sparge the grains.
4) Press in 25 g/1 oz of hops, cover the pan and boil for 1 hour. Press in the rest of the hops and boil for another 15 minutes.
5) Leave to stand for 30 minutes, then strain out the hops through a sparging bag into a polythene bin.
6) Stir in the glucose, top up with cold water and leave to cool. Check the specific gravity; it should be between 1.090 and 1.100. If it is too low, adjust the level by adding more sugar; if it is too high, add more water until the required reading is obtained.
7) Pitch the activated ale yeast, then ferment, skim and stir for 4 days.
8) Siphon the wine into a storage jar, add the activated Champagne yeast, fit an airlock and ferment out.
9) Rack into beer bottles, prime with caster sugar at the rate of 5 ml/1 tsp per 1 litre/2 pints barley wine then seal and label.
10) Mature for at least 1 year before drinking.

Beer must be both clear and have a good head. The beer on the extreme left of this picture is clear but flat while that on the right is both cloudy and flat. Only the beer in the centre is suitable for drinking.

AVOIDING AND SOLVING PROBLEMS

Beer is subject to few problems, especially if good hygiene is maintained and good ingredients are used.

The few problems that can occur can be categorized as follows:

1) **Flat beer.** If there is no life in the beer when it is poured, the cause is either insufficient priming or an imperfect seal. Re-prime and re-seal and leave for one week.

2) **Gush.** If the beer gushes forth in foam when the bottle is opened, the cause is either too much priming or bottling before fermentation is finished. Pour the beer into a bin and when the foam has cleared, bottle it again, using minimum priming.

3) **Off flavours.** Unpleasant smells and tastes, including vinegar taint, are due to poor ingredients, dirty equipment or leaving the beer exposed to the air. There is no cure and the beer should be discarded.

4) **Yeast bite.** A bitterness develops in the beer if the froth is not skimmed and the beer roused during fermentation. Clean off the yeast ring also. Rack the beer when fermentation is finished. Also ferment at the correct temperature.

OTHER DRINKS

MEAD

There is no doubt that mead was the first fermented drink tasted by man. Made from wild honey dissolved in water, left for a little while, possibly accidentally, and then probably drunk while still fermenting, mead must have been sufficiently unusual for our forebears of 12,000 years ago to have repeated the process of making it deliberately.

Ingredients

Honey. Two kinds are available – one which is creamy fawn in colour with a firm consistency, and the other which is a rich brown, runny honey. A light honey is suitable for dry and delicate meads with their subtle flavours, while dark honey tends to make a less pleasant dry mead on its own, and is best used in conjunction with spices or fruits to make a sweet and strong mead.

Honey is formed from the nectar collected from flowers by bees, and taken to their hive for storage and winter food. It consists of 77% sugar and 17½% water. The remaining 5½% includes salts of iron, lime, manganese phosphorus, potassium, sodium and sulphate, together with some traces of acids, pollen, vitamins, waxes etc.

The kinds of flowers from which the nectar is extracted, affect the flavour of honey, and consequently the mead. Californian or Spanish orange blossom honey makes a delicious dry mead in which the flavour of the oranges can be faintly detected. English honey, although expensive, is, however, generally rated the best in the world and is worth using if you can get hold of enough. Canadian clover honey is good for making sweet meads.

Acid, tannin and nutrient. As honey contains virtually none of these, it is important to add sufficient quantities to obtain a good fermentation and flavour.

Yeast. This is used in the same way as for wines (see page 18).

General Method

Because natural honey contains minute quantities of wax and unwanted ingredients, it is best to dissolve it in warm water and then to bring it slowly just to the simmering point. Never boil the must since this drives off some of the very flavours that are needed. The scum that rises should be skimmed as it forms and the clear solution covered and cooled as quickly as possible.

When the must is cool, an activated yeast, citric acid, nutrient, tannin and any other ingredients should be stirred in and the must poured into a fermentation jar. An airlock should be fitted and the jar stood in a warm place until fermentation has finished.

Mead is sometimes slow in fermenting and it is essential to keep it in an even temperature of about 21°C/70°F until fermentation has finished. This may take as long as six months. It should then be processed in the same way as wine as far as racking, bottling and storing is concerned (see pages 20–23). It can also be made into a sparkling mead in the same way as a sparkling wine (see pages 25–26).

Serving Mead

Mead should always be served crisp and cool; even table mead tastes better just off dry rather than very dry. A single saccharin tablet per bottle is sufficient to take the hard edge off a very dry mead.

DRY MEAD

1.5 kg/3 lb light honey
3.75 litres/7½ pints water
20 ml/4 tsps citric acid
2.5 ml/½ tsp nutrient
1.25 ml/¼ tsp grape tannin
activated Maury or sherry flor wine yeast
1 Campden tablet

1) Dissolve the honey in some warm water and when it has dissolved, top up with cold water. Check the specific gravity; it should read about 1.085. Add more honey or water as necessary to achieve this gravity. If you have no more honey, white sugar may be used to adjust the gravity.
2) Bring the must slowly to simmering point, then skim, cover and leave to cool.
3) Stir in the acid, nutrient, tannin and yeast, and pour the must into a fermentation jar. Fit an airlock and leave it in a warm place to ferment out.
4) Siphon the mead into a sterilized storage jar, top up if necessary, add the Campden tablet, bung tight, label and store for 6 weeks.
5) Rack again when it is bright, and mature in bulk for 1 year. If hazy after the 6 weeks, fine and rack again after 1 week.
6) Bottle and store for 6 months. Serve as for a white wine.

SWEET MEAD

2.25 kg/4½ lb dark honey
3 litres/6 pints warm water
25 g/1 oz citric acid
2.5 ml/½ tsp nutrient
2.5 ml/½ tsp grape tannin
activated Maury or Sauternes wine yeast
1 Campden tablet
1.25 ml/¼ tsp potassium sorbate

1) Dissolve half the honey in the water.
2) Bring the must slowly to simmering point, then skim, cover and leave to cool.
3) Stir in the acid, nutrient, tannin and yeast, then pour the must into a fermentation jar, leaving space for the rest of the honey. Fit an airlock and leave the must to ferment until the specific gravity has fallen to 1.010.
4) Stir in half the remaining honey, re-fit the airlock and continue the fermentation until the specific gravity has again fallen to 1.010.
5) Stir in the remaining honey and continue checking the gravity at periodic intervals until the reading is 1.020.
6) Rack the must into a sterilized storage jar, add the Campden tablet and potassium sorbate, re-fit the airlock and store in a cool, dry place until bright. Rack again if necessary.
7) Store for 1 year before bottling this sweet, honey-tasting mead. Serve cold, with sweet biscuits.

MELOMEL

1.5 kg/3 lb light honey
2.75 litres/5¾ pints water
1 litre/2 pints orange juice
2.5 ml/½ tsp nutrient
activated Maury or general purpose yeast
1 Campden tablet

1) Dissolve the honey in 1 litre/2 pints warm water. Add the remaining cold water, then stir in the orange juice, nutrient and activated yeast.
2) Pour the must into a fermentation jar, top up with cold water, fit an airlock and leave in a warm place to ferment out.
3) Siphon the clearing melomel into a sterilized storage jar, top up, add 1 Campden tablet, bung tight, label and store until bright.
4) Rack again and mature in bulk for 1 year.
5) Rack into bottles, sweetening to taste with saccharin. Serve cold as a white wine.

Note No extra acid is required. There is enough in the orange juice.

VARIATIONS

Use fruit juices such as pineapple, apricot, blackcurrant, grapefruit or passion-fruit instead of the orange juice.
Cyser
Substitute apple juice for the orange juice.
Pyment
Use grape juice instead of the orange juice.
Metheglin
Infuse such spices as 1 ginger root, 12 cloves and a cinnamon stick while the must is fermenting. Leave for about 4 days, then remove from the clearing wine.

This mead has a splendid flavour when served hot at 60°C/140°F.

GINGER BEER

25 g/1 oz dried ginger root, bruised
thinly pared and chopped rind and juice of 1 lemon
15 g/½ oz cream of tartar
250 g/8 oz white sugar
4.4 litres/9 pints boiling water
activated beer yeast

1) Place the ginger root in a polythene bin with the lemon rind, cream of tartar and the sugar.
2) Pour the boiling water over these ingredients, stir well to dissolve the sugar, cover and leave overnight to cool.
3) Add the expressed and strained lemon juice and the yeast. Replace the cover and leave in a warm place.
4) Next day, skim off the dirty froth, stir the brew, replace the cover and leave in a warm place to ferment out. Skim again.
5) Rack into beer bottles, sweeten to taste with saccharin, seal as for beer (see page 60), then label and store for a few days while fermentation finishes in the bottles.
6) Chill the bottles in a refrigerator and serve cold.

Note Do not add more sugar than that mentioned, nor bottle the beer before the end of the third day since this may cause an excess of carbon dioxide in the bottles that could be dangerous.

Alternatively, ferment out all the sugar, sweeten with saccharin and prime with caster sugar as for beer (see page 60).

The quantity of ginger beer obtained from this recipe is 9 × 500 ml/16 fl oz bottles.

CIDER

When apple juice is fermented, the resulting beverage is called cider. The juice is pressed out of a mixture of crushed apples picked from varieties of trees grown exclusively for the production of cider.

The popularity of cider is increasing to such an extent that cans of cider concentrate can now be bought in home-brew centres. Step-by-step instructions are given on the label and an attractive cider can be easily and quickly made at home in the same way as wine and beer from kits.

More adventurous people may like to make cider from their surplus apples. It is important to use a mixture of apples roughly in the proportion of four parts sweet apples to two parts sour and one part bitter. This blend of sugar, acid and tannin produces a much more balanced beverage than one made from any single variety. The problem of using only one variety of apple can be partially overcome by the addition as necessary of sugar, malic acid and grape tannin, together with some cider concentrate, in much the same way as grape juice concentrate is added to fruit and other country wines. No water is needed.

72

DRY STILL CIDER

A satisfactory cider can be made with the following apples. It is important, however, that all of them should be mellowed.

6 kg/12 lb eating apples (Cox, Fortune, Golden Delicious)
3 kg/6 lb cooking apples (Bramley, Blenheim, Derby)
1 kg/2 lb hard pears or crabapples (Conference,
   John Downie)
Campden tablets as required
pectic enzyme as required
sugar as required
activated Champagne wine yeast

1) Wash the apples thoroughly clean of leaves, grass and soil. Bruised and damaged portions should be removed to avoid an oxidized flavour in the finished cider.
2) Crush or pulp the apples as efficiently and quickly as possible, and press them without delay to avoid oxidation of the fruit and juice.
3) Add 1 crushed Campden tablet and 5 ml/1 tsp pectic enzyme for every 5 kg/10 lb crushed fruit.
4) Pour the juice into a fermentation jar, fit an airlock and leave it in a warm place for 24 hours while the enzyme works.
5) Measure the specific gravity and stir in sufficient sugar if necessary to bring the reading up to 1.046.
6) Add the yeast and ferment slowly at a temperature of around 15°C/59°F to maintain the fruit flavour.
7) When fermentation has finished, rack the cider into a storage jar, add 1 Campden tablet, bung tight, label and store in a cold place until bright, then rack again.
8) Siphon into bottles and mature for 4–6 months.

Note The inclusion of 250 g/8 oz cider concentrate per 5 litres/5 quarts juice at the start of fermentation improves the cider flavour.

VARIATION

Sparkling cider can be made in exactly the same way as sparkling wine (see pages 25–26).

SWEET CIDER

6 kg/12 lb eating apples (Cox, Fortune, Golden Delicious)
3 kg/6 lb cooking apples (Bramley, Blenheim, Derby)
1 kg/2 lb hard pears or crabapples (Conference,
   John Downie)
Campden tablets as required
pectic enzyme as required
sugar as required
activated Champagne wine yeast
1.25 ml/¼ tsp potassium sorbate

1) Wash the apples thoroughly, then crush or pulp them, and press quickly.
2) Add 1 crushed Campden tablet and 5 ml/1 tsp pectic enzyme for every 5 kg/10 lb crushed fruit.
3) Pour the juice into a fermentation jar, fit an airlock and leave in a warm place for 24 hours.
4) Measure the specific gravity and stir in sufficient sugar to bring the reading up to 1.060.
5) Add the yeast and ferment slowly at a temperature of around 15°C/59°F.
6) When the gravity falls to 1.010, add another Campden tablet and the potassium sorbate.
7) Rack in a storage jar, bung tight, label and store in a cold place until bright, then rack again.
8) Siphon into bottles, and mature for 4–6 months.

Above right Crushing apples with a mallet before pressing them.

Right Pressing apple pulp to obtain juice. This must be done immediately after crushing the apples to avoid oxidation of the fruit and juice.

Very palatable liqueurs can be made easily and cheaply, although they are, of course, more expensive than home-made wines.

Only four main ingredients are necessary – sweet strong wine, vodka, caster sugar and a Noirot liqueur flavouring of your choice.

The wine base should lack any pronounced flavour; its colour should obviously be related to the colour of the liqueur.

Vodka increases the alcoholic strength of the liqueur, and because it is flavourless, does not clash with the chosen essence.

175 g/6 oz caster sugar
475 ml/16 fl oz strong sweet wine
275 ml/19 fl oz vodka (approximately 80 proof)
20 ml/4 tsp Noirot flavouring essence

1) Put the sugar in a jug, and add the wine and vodka to dissolve it, then stir in about 15 ml/3 tsps of the flavouring.
2) Taste the liqueur and add a little more flavouring, sugar or vodka as desired. It is so much easier to add more and so difficult to adjust the balance once too much of any one ingredient has been used.
3) The liqueur can be much improved with 10–15 ml/2–3 tsps of glycerine and 12–15 drops of capsicum tincture added just before bottling. The glycerine adds smoothness and richness; the capsicum adds warmth and character. Although not essential, they are well worth including. The liqueur is immediately ready for drinking.

Note The colourless French *eau-de-vie* may be substituted for vodka in liqueurs such as apricot brandy, cherry brandy and peach brandy.

This recipe produces 800 ml/27 fl oz of liqueur.

SLOE GIN

375 g/12 oz fresh sloes, stalked, washed and drained
125 g/4 oz sugar
1 × 75 cl/25.6 fl oz bottle gin

1) Prick the berries with a needle or fork so that the juice can escape, then pack them into a screw-topped jar.
2) Dissolve the sugar in the gin and pour it over the sloes.
3) Screw on the lid and seal the jar, then shake it gently to mix the gin, sugar and fruit.
4) Store in a dark place for 3 months, shaking the jar occasionally to distribute the colour and flavour.
5) Strain off the liquor, then bottle. Store for 3 months.
Note If eating the sloes, beware of the stones.

ORANGE GIN

rind of 1 Seville orange and 1 lemon, thinly pared and chopped
1 × 75 cl/25.6 fl oz bottle gin
125 g/4 oz sugar

1) Place the chopped rind in a 1 litre/2 pint bottle, together with the gin and the sugar.
2) Cork the bottle and shake gently to dissolve the sugar.
3) Store for 1 week, shaking daily, then remove the rind and bottle the liqueur.
Note Orange gin improves when kept for some months.

GLOSSARY OF TERMS

Acid An essential ingredient in fermented beverages. Several acids may be present in a wine must, such as citric, malic or tartaric, and others such as propionic, succinic or valerianic are produced during fermentation. Yeast needs an acid solution in which to grow and thrive. Wine needs acid to enhance the bouquet and impart freshness to the flavour.

Activate To change yeast cells from a dormant condition to an active one in which they are able to reproduce themselves and ferment sugar. This occurs when yeast is dissolved in a dilute acid and sugar solution.

Adjuncts Ingredients added to malt and hops to increase the alcohol content and improve the body and flavour of the beer. The most popular are torrified barley, flaked maize, flaked rice and wheat flour. Sugar, too, is an adjunct.

Airlock A device for excluding air from a fermenting must while still enabling the carbon dioxide produced in a fermentation to escape into the atmosphere. Also called fermentation lock or trap.

Alcohol A spiritous substance produced during the fermentation of sugar. There are many alcohols such as amyl, butyl and methyl which are dangerously toxic when consumed in more than minute quantities. For all winemaking and brewing purposes we are mainly concerned with ethyl alcohol, sometimes called ethanol. It is this spirit that makes beers, ciders, meads and wines so enjoyable and satisfying.

Aldehydes The product of the partial oxidation of alcohol. The best known is acetaldehyde which is formed from ethyl alcohol during fermentation. It contributes towards the bouquet and characteristic flavour of wine.

Ammonium phosphate/sulphate Mineral salts added to a must to provide a source of nitrogen for the yeast, without which it cannot thrive. Also referred to as yeast nutrient.

Barley The grain from which most beers are made. It is first moistened and warmed to stimulate growth and the production of enzymes. When growth has produced far enough to break down the substance protecting the starch, it is stopped by heating the grain to 50°C/122°F for a period. This produces a pale malt as the barley is now called. Heating to a higher temperature produces crystal malt, chocolate malt or black malt, each of which contributes a different flavour in the beer.

Bentonite A volcanic clay used as a fining agent. Available in the form of a gel or as granules which are easier to disperse.

Body The fullness of a wine or beer. A full bodied beverage is the opposite of a thin one.

Bung A large rubber or cork stopper used for sealing a storage jar.

Campden tablet A compressed quantity of sodium metabisulphite weighing 0.45 g which releases 50 ppm of sulphur dioxide when dissolved in 5 litres/1 gallon of must or wine. It is a powerful bactericide and anti-oxidant.

Cap The solid ingredients in a pulp fermentation that are raised to the surface and above by the bubbles of carbon dioxide produced by the yeast from the fruit sugar. The cap must be kept submerged or pressed down twice daily so that its soluble constituents can be extracted.

Capsicum tincture A liquid produced from the capsicum (green pepper) plant. It burns the tongue if tasted and adds a warm glow to liqueurs.

Carbon dioxide (CO_2) A by-product of the fermentation of sugar into alcohol. This colourless and odourless gas rises to the surface of a fermenting must in the form of countless bubbles each of which bursts with a slight hissing sound.

Dextrin A member of the sugar family; produced when malted barley is steeped in hot water.

Diammonium phosphate A mineral salt that releases nitrogen when dissolved in water. Often called a yeast nutrient since the yeast cell needs nitrogen to remain active.

Disgorgement The removal of the sediment from a bottle of sparkling wine, prior to serving.

Eau-de-vie A spirit produced from the distillation of wine. The base may be grapes or other fruits, grains or potatoes.

End point The moment in time when all the starch in malted barley that is being steeped in hot water has been converted to sugars.

Ferment out To ferment a must until no sugar remains unconverted.

Fermentation The reduction of sugar into alcohol and carbon dioxide by the enzymes secreted by yeast.

Fermentation jar A glass vessel with a narrow neck supported by two carrying rings. It has a nominal capacity of 5 litres/1 gallon.

Fermentation on the pulp The fermentation of sugar in the presence of crushed fruit. The useful constituents of the fruit are extracted by being soaked in water, and the movement thereby caused is a result of bubbles of carbon dioxide and the formation of a small quantity of alcohol in which some substances are more readily soluble.

Fermentation trap See **Airlock.**

Filtering The removal of suspended solids from a liquid by passing them through a cellulose pad or powder.

Finings Substances that attract the suspended solids when added to a hazy beverage, and which cause them to sink to the bottom of the container, thus leaving the liquid above clear and bright. Isinglass, bentonite and gelatine are commonly used.

Flor A white or creamy skin of fungi that develops in the presence of air on the surface of a wine or beer. There are several kinds:

1) Flowers of wine (*Mycoderma vini*). This forms on wine or beer in containers which have been inadequately sealed. The fungi attacks the alcohol and reduces it to carbon dioxide and water.

2) Mother of vinegar (*Mycoderma aceti*). This forms on low alcohol wines, beers or ciders that are left open to the air. The alcohol is converted into acetic acid.

3) Sherry flor. A combination of micro-organisms that develop on strong sherry wines with access to air. The wine is oxidized and acetaldehyde is formed, producing the distinctive sherry bouquet and taste.

Fortification The addition of alcohol to a wine to make it stronger, eg sherry and port type wines.

Glucose A single sugar commonly found in grapes. Frequently used as an additive to a wort in the brewing of beer. Also used in winemaking.

Glycerine A colourless, oily liquid added to a liqueur to impart smoothness.

Hardening salts A combination of calcium sulphate (gypsum) and magnesium sulphate (Epsom salts) with traces of calcium chloride and sodium chloride. Used for adding to soft water when brewing bitter beers, strong ales and barley wines.

Haze A film of suspended solids dispersed throughout a wine, beer or cider.

Hops The flowers of the *Humulus lupulus*. They are used for flavouring and preserving beer.

Hydrometer An instrument for measuring the density or weight of liquid compared with the weight of water at 15°C/59°F. Commonly used in winemaking and brewing for ascertaining both the sugar content and potential alcohol content of a must or wort. Also called a saccharometer.

Isinglass A fining agent produced from the swim bladder of certain fish.

Lactose A sugar that cannot be fermented by wine or beer yeast. It is most frequently used for sweetening brown ales and stouts. It is only one-third as sweet as household sugar.

Lees The collection of dead yeast cells, particles of pulp and other solids that form on the bottom of a container, during and immediately after fermentation. Also called sediment.

Macerate The process of expressing the flavour from flowers by rubbing them against a hard surface with the back of a wooden spoon while they are being steeped in water.

Maltose The sugar produced by the diastatic enzymes from the starch in the barley grains. It is subsequently converted into glucose by the enzyme called maltose.

Mash To infuse grains or fruits in water to extract colour, flavour, sugar, acids, minerals, vitamins etc.

Mashing vessel A polythene or stainless steel bucket or bin in which malted barley and other grains are steeped in hot water. Also used for pulp fermentation of fruit wines.

Maturation The period of storage after fermentation when a wine, beer, mead or cider undergoes subtle chemical changes until it reaches its most pleasing taste. The length of period varies with each individual brew and no firm guidance can be given. In general, light beverages mature more quickly than stronger ones.

Mead The product of the fermentation of a honey solution.

Metabisulphite See **Campden tablet**.

Méthode Champenoise The method by which sparkling wine is made, ie refermentation in the bottle.

Must The name given to a liquid with or without pulp prepared for fermentation into wine.

Noirot The trade name of liqueur essences from France.

Nutrient One or more ammonium salts sometimes combined with vitamin B_1 that is added to a must to provide yeast cells with nitrogen.

Oxidize The browning of fruit when it is cut and exposed to the air. A similar action occurs when a fermented beverage is exposed to the air. The result is a dull, flat taste that lacks appeal.

Pectic enzyme Sometimes described as 'pectolytic enzyme' or sold under brand names. It is a combination of enzymes in powder or liquid form that dissolve the pectin in fruit, thereby improving the juice extraction and ensuring also a haze-free wine or cider.

pH The measure of the acidity of a beverage as opposed to the total acid content. Some acids are more tart than others and what we taste is the tartness of the acid, not the quantity present. pH is measured from 0–14, ranging from maximum acidity at 0 to maximum alkalinity at 14, with a neutral point at about 7. The optimum for wine and mead is from 3.2 to 3.4, for beer from 5 to 5.4 and for cider from 4 to 4.4.

Pitch The action of adding yeast to a wort.

Potassium sorbate A substance used in conjunction with metabisulphite to terminate the fermentation of a must, thus leaving a residue of sugar.

Priming The addition of a small quantity of sugar to a wine or beer to cause a secondary fermentation in the bottle.

The carbon dioxide produced gives effervescence and vitality to the wine or beer when it is poured.

Racking The removal of a clear or clearing beverage from a sediment after fermentation. Usually performed with the aid of a siphon.

Rouse To stir up a fermenting beverage to release carbon dioxide and admit oxygen so that the yeast cells can reproduce themselves and continue the fermentation.

Saccharometer See **Hydrometer**.

Sediment See **Lees**.

Siphon A plastic or rubber tube used for transferring a beverage from one vessel to another.

Sodium metabisulphite See **Campden tablet**.

Sparging The rinsing of grains with warm water in beer making after they have been mashed, to wash off any remaining traces of maltose.

Specific gravity The weight or density of a liquid compared with the same volume of water at 15°C/59°F. See also **Hydrometer**.

Spoilage organisms Bacteria, fungi and moulds that feed on exposed fermenting or fermented beverages and impart an unpleasant smell and taste that spoils the beverage.

Starter An activated yeast ready for mixing into a must. The yeast is usually re-activated in a weak sugar and acid solution containing nutrient.

Sulphite The widely used abbreviation of sodium or potassium metabisulphite. See also **Campden tablet**.

Sulphur dioxide The gas released when sulphite is dissolved in a liquid. It is a powerful bactericide and anti-oxidant.

Tannin A substance found in the skin and stalks of certain fruits, notably black grapes. It adds a hint of bitterness, firmness and character to wine, mead and cider. It is advisable to add a small quantity of grape tannin to most musts.

Tartrates Crystal-like substances formed by the interaction of tartaric acid and mineral salts. They precipitate in alcoholic beverages at low temperatures.

Trial jar A tall plastic or glass cylinder in which the specific gravity of a liquid is measured with a hydrometer.

Wort The name of a hopped malt solution prior to fermentation into beer.

Yeast nutrient See **Ammonium phosphate**.

INDEX

Note All recipe entries are in italic, eg *Apple table wine 29*